For Reference

Not to be taken from this room

RIBBONS
of Orders, Decorations and Medals

Other books by Guido Rosignoli

Army Badges and Insignia
of World War II, Book I.
Great Britain, Poland, Belgium,
Italy, USSR, USA, Germany.

Army Badges and Insignia
of World War II, Book II.
Canada, South Africa, India,
Finland, France, Japan,
Netherlands, Yugoslavia, China,
Denmark, Czechoslovakia.

Army Badges and Insignia
Since 1945, Book I.
Great Britain, Poland, USA,
Italy, German Federal
and Democratic Republics,
USSR, Belgium.

Ribbons of Orders, Decorations and Medals

by
Guido Rosignoli

ARCO PUBLISHING COMPANY, INC.
New York

Published 1977 by Arco Publishing Company, Inc.
219 Park Avenue South, New York, N.Y. 10003

Copyright © Blandford Press 1976

All rights reserved

Printed in Great Britain

Library of Congress Cataloging in Publication Data

Rosignoli, Guido.
  Ribbons of orders, decorations, and medals.

  (Arco color series)
  Includes index.
  1. Decorations of honor. 2. Orders of knighthood and chivalry—Insignia. 3. Medals. I. Title.
CR4661.R67   929.7   76–28307
ISBN 0–668–04104–8
ISBN 0–668–04253–2 pbk

To
Licio Granata

Contents

Introduction	9
Acknowledgements	11
The Illustrations	13
Descriptive Text	77
Belgium (Plates 1–2)	77
Czechoslovak Socialist Republic (Plates 3–5)	80
Kingdom of Denmark (Plate 6)	85
Republic of France (Plates 7–14)	86
German Empire (Plate 15)	98
German Third Reich (Plates 16–18)	100
German Democratic Republic (Plate 19)	104
German Federal Republic (Plate 20)	105
Great Britain (Plates 22–31)	107
People's Republic of Hungary (Plates 32–3)	124
Empire of Iran (Plate 34)	126
Kingdom of Italy (Plates 35–40)	126
Italian Republic (Plates 40–1)	134
Kingdom of the Netherlands (Plate 42)	136
Kingdom of Norway (Plate 43)	137
Republic of Poland (Plates 44–5)	138
Polish People's Republic (Plates 45–7)	141
Imperial Russia (Plate 48)	142
Union of the Soviet Socialist Republics (Plates 49–53)	145
United States of America (Plates 54–8)	149
Republic of Vietnam (Plates 59–60)	158
Kingdom of Yugoslavia (Plates 61–2)	160
Socialist Federal Republic of Yugoslavia (Plates 63–4)	163
Bibliographical Note	165

Introduction

Although at first I was not particularly interested in ribbons I have added to my collection from time to time for over twenty years. But the home of my ribbons was an old cardboard box.

I tried a few times to set them in some sort of order on panels, but eventually found that all my time had been wasted because some should have had badges or rosettes attached in the centre and many were inevitably missing. As no available publication seemed able to help me in my task and as, obviously, many fellow collectors would be in the same predicament, I decided to study this subject thoroughly and make the result of my research into a book.

This book deals mainly with service ribbons, worn on their own on the breast, although general information on the decorations and medals they represent is also included in the text. Some of the ribbons illustrated, mainly of civilian awards, are not worn in the form of service ribbons as the medal, with its suspension ribbon, is worn at all times but should be included, as otherwise possessors of these ribbons will not know what they are.

Therefore in each chapter I have dealt with all the ribbons of a nation or, of a specific period, including the classes of the orders of knighthood, decorations and medals, and the various badges and devices which could be worn on their ribbons. If the text, as a whole, seems unbalanced it is because I have more information on the ribbons of some countries than on those of others and the pattern of my information varies too. Space limitations have compelled me to reduce the descriptive text to an indispensable minimum as the knowledgeable reader will realise that I could have written several thousand pages on the ribbons of some nations. Other forms of criticism are inevitable; rightly an associate has already mentioned there was no point in wasting valuable space with certain orders which monarchs and presidents exchange among themselves, as their ribbons can never be found. Some historically minded collectors are only interested in campaign medals and will consider that I should, at least, have ignored the civilian awards in order to include some 'better' ribbons of a few other nations. But, in my opinion, some of these modest civilian medals represent a lifetime's work, or the bravery of a fireman, or a casual passerby's action to save someone's life at the risk of his or her own.

Why should the officer get a cross while the soldier, for the same deed, gets only a medal? Why are the ribbons of some generals covered by citation badges while soldiers who endured years of campaigning have none? Biting questions that have no answer.

The ribbons and decorations have been illustrated in actual size and are reduced by one third in the printing process, thus the illustrations are one third smaller than the original items. However, often the same ribbon can be found in different widths, in slightly different colours, due to manufacture, and also in different lengths depending on the fashion of the day or other circumstances. Innumerable regulations, modified over and over again, rule the wearing of service ribbons and, due to this fact or simple carelessness, many ribbons are incorrectly placed on ribbon bars.

The order of precedence of wearing these ribbons is far too complicated a subject to deal with in the number of pages at my disposal; the army, navy and air force each have their own order of precedence, although many of their ribbons are the same.

If any of my readers wish to specialize in collecting the ribbons of one country in particular they will have to continue and deepen my research. I sincerely hope that this book will prove a useful start.

G. Rosignoli,
Farnham, Surrey, 1976

Acknowledgments

I would like to thank:

Major E. R. Davreux.
The Embassy of the Czechoslovak Socialist Republic.
Captain P. J. Jorgensen and Mrs Inga Fl. Rasmussen.
Mr D. C. Bartlett.
The Embassy of the Federal Republic of Germany, Mr A. Mollo, Mr. F. Ollenschläger and Mr P. Preuss of Steinhauer & Lück, Lüdenscheid.
Mr A. L. Kipling, Major A. G. Brown, M.B.E., Curator of the Royal Marines Museum and Mr Peter F. King.
The Embassy of the Hungarian People's Republic.
The Imperial Iranian Embassy and the Headquarters of the Imperial Iranian Armed Forces, at Teheran.
The Embassy of Italy, Geom. L. Granata and Prof. L. Verni.
Captain H. Ringoir, Hon. Gunner of the R.N.A.
Mr A. Kielland Hauge, Curator of the Hærmuseet, Oslo.
Mr K. Barbarski, Vice-curator of the Polish Institute and Sikorski Museum.
The Embassy of the U.S.S.R.
The U.S. Department of the Navy, Office of Information and the Headquarters U.S. Marine Corps, Mr Pierre C. T. Verheye.
The Embassy of the Republic of Vietnam.
The Embassy of the Socialist Federal Republic of Yugoslavia.
Lieut.-Colonel P. M. Pavasovic, President of the Royal Yugoslav ex-Combatants Association 'Drazha Mihailovic' and Mr Milan P. Pavasovic.

My most sincere thanks to my wife Diana who patiently transformed my manuscript into the text of this book.

KINGDOM OF BELGIUM

ORDERS AND DECORATIONS

PLATE 1

KINGDOM OF BELGIUM

WAR MEDALS

20 1870–71
21 Volontaires 1914–18
22 Yser
23 Décoration Maritime 1914–18
24 Médaille de la Reine Elisabeth
25 Médaille du Roi Albert
26 Campagne d'Afrique 1914–16
29 Croix du Feu
30 Prisonniers Politiques 1914–18
31 Déportés 1914–18
32 Médaille Interalliée 1914–18
33 Croix de Guerre 1941
34 Médaille Commémorative 1940–45
35 Volontaires 1940–45
27 Croix de Guerre 1914–18
28 Médaille Commémorative 1914–18
37 Prisonniers Politiques 1940–45
38 Prisonniers de Guerre 1940–45
47 Médaille Commémorative T.O.E. (Corée)
36 Médaille Maritime 1940–45
40 Résistance
41 Résistance Civil
48 Indépendance 1830–1930
39 Réfractaire 1940–45
42 Évadés
43 Abyssinie 1941
46 Reconnaissance Belge
44 Médaille Africaine de la Guerre 1940–45
45 Effort de la Guerre Colonial
49 Commémorative Roi Albert

PLATE 2

CZECHOSLOVAK SOCIALIST REPUBLIC

ORDERS, DECORATIONS AND MEDALS

2 Zlatá hvězda hrdiny ČSSR

1 Řád Klementa Gottwalda
-za budování socialistické vlasti

3 Zlatá hvězda hrdiny socialistické práce

6 Stužka laureáta státní ceny Klementa Gottwalda

7 Čs. státní novinářská cena václava kopeckého

8 I. stupeň vyznamenání 'Za zásluhy 10 let Lidových milicí'

9 II. stupeň vyznamenání 'Za zásluhy 10 let Lidových milicí'

10 Řád rudého praporu práce

4 Stříbrna hvězda

11 Řád rudé hvězdy práce

12 Vyznamenání Za pracovní věrnost

5 Stříbrna/bronzová medaile Řádu 25 února 1948

13 Vyznamenání Za pracovní Obětavost

PLATE 3

CZECHOSLOVAK SOCIALIST REPUBLIC

DECORATIONS AND MEDALS

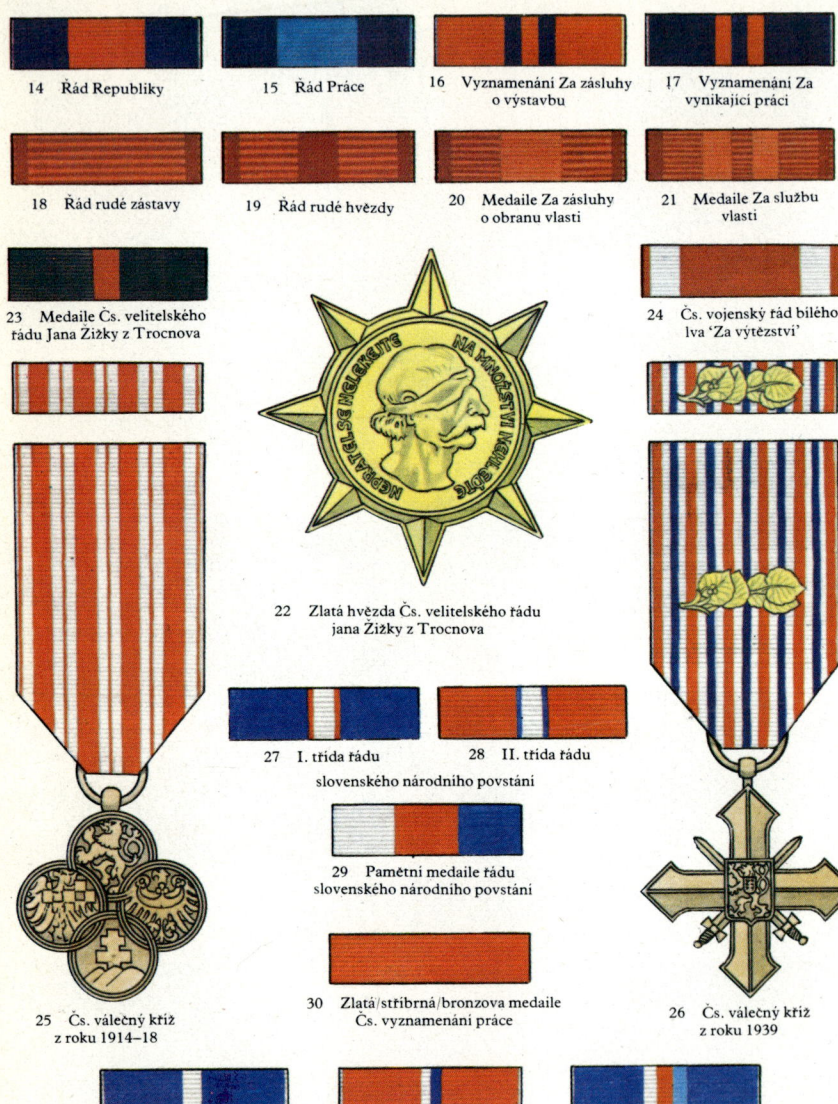

14 Řád Republiky
15 Řád Práce
16 Vyznamenání Za zásluhy o výstavbu
17 Vyznamenání Za vynikající práci
18 Řád rudé zástavy
19 Řád rudé hvězdy
20 Medaile Za zásluhy o obranu vlasti
21 Medaile Za službu vlasti
22 Zlatá hvězda Čs. velitelského řádu jana Žižky z Trocnova
23 Medaile Čs. velitelského řádu Jana Žižky z Trocnova
24 Čs. vojenský řád bílého lva 'Za vítězství'
25 Čs. válečný kříž z roku 1914–18
26 Čs. válečný kříž z roku 1939
27 I. třída řádu
28 II. třída řádu slovenského národního povstání
29 Pamětní medaile řádu slovenského národního povstání
30 Zlatá/stříbrná/bronzová medaile Čs. vyznamenání práce
31 Vyznamenání medaile J. E. Purkyně
32 Vyznamenání medaile J. A. Komenského
33 Vyznamenání Za statečnost

PLATE 4

CZECHOSLOVAK SOCIALIST REPUBLIC

DECORATIONS AND MEDALS

35 Stříbrná/bronzová medaile
Čs. vojenského řádu 'Za svobodu'

37 Čs. Jánošikova medaile

39 Sokolovská pamětní medaile

41 Bachmačská pamětní medaile

43 Čs. vojenska pamětní medaile

45 Čs. revoluční medaile

34 Zlatá hvězda
Čs. vojenského řádu 'Za svobodu'

47 Odznak Čs. partyzána

36 Čs. medaile Za chrabrost před nepřítelem

38 Čs. vojenská medaile Za zásluhy stříbrná/bronzova

40 Zborovská pamětní medaile

42 Dukelska pamětní medaile

44 Pamětni odznak druhého národního odboje

46 Pamětní odznak osvobozených politických vězňů

48 I. třida-Čs. řád bilého lva

PLATE 5

KINGDOM OF DENMARK

ORDERS, DECORATIONS AND MEDALS

1 Elefantordenen

4 Fortjenstmedaljen

2 Dannebrogordenen Ridder

5 Krigsmindemedaille 1848–50 og 1864

6 Eringdringsmedaille for deltagense i krigen 1940–45

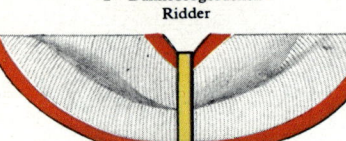

7 Hæderstegn for god tjeneste

8 For god tjeneste i politiet

9 For god tjeneste i civilforsvaret

10 Hjemmeværnets fortjensttegn

11 Medaljen for udmærket lufttjeneste

12 For god tjeneste brandvæsenet

13 Eringdringstegn i anledning af Kong Christian IX og Dronning Louises Guldbryllup

14 Den slesvigske eringdringsmedaille af 1920

3 Dannebrogordenen Kommandør

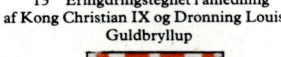
16 Reserveofficersforeningen i Danmarks Hæderstegn

15 Koreamedaillen

17 Civilforsvars-Forgundets hæderstegn

19 Håndværksrådets hæderstegn

20 Dansk Røte Kors' Hæderstegn -Medaille

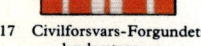
18 Turistforeningen for Danmark's hæderstegn

22 Dansk Røte Kors' mindetegn for krigsfangeudvekslingen i Korea 1953

21 Dansk Røte Kors' mindetegn for Krigsfangehjælp

PLATE 6

REPUBLIC OF FRANCE

ORDERS AND DECORATIONS

2 Grand Croix

3 Grand Officier

7 Croix de la Libération

9 Croix de Guerre
   1914–18

11 Croix de Guerre
    1939–45

12 Croix de Guerre
    avec citations

13 Croix de Guerre
    1939–40

1 Légion d'Honneur
4 Commandeur

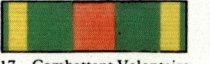
17 Combattant Volontaire

18 Évadés

19 Résistance

20 Combattant Volontaire
    Résistant

21 22 Services Militaires Volontaires
    or-argent   bronze

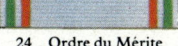
23 Reconnaissance
    Française

24 Ordre du Mérite
    de l'Afrique Noire

5 Officier

6 Chevalier

8 Médaille Militaire

10 Croix de Guerre
    T.O.E.

14 Croix du Combattant

15 Croix du Combattant

16 Croix du Combattant
    1939–40

PLATE 7

REPUBLIC OF FRANCE

ORDERS OF MERIT

26 Mérite Agricole
27 Mérite Commercial
28 Santé Publique
29 Mérite Artisanal
31 Mérite Maritime Chevalier
32 Mérite Social Officier
25 Ordre National du Mérite Commandeur
30 Mérite Maritime Officier
34 Palmes Académiques
33 Mérite Social Chevalier
35 Mérite Turistique
36 Mérite Combattant
37 Mérite Postal
38 Économie Nationale
39 Mérite Sportif
40 Mérite du Travail
41 Mérite Militaire
42 Mérite Civil
43 Arts et Lettres
44 Mérite Saharien
45 Mérite National

PLATE 8

REPUBLIC OF FRANCE

WAR MEDALS

46 Crimea
47 Baltic
48 Médaille de Chine
49 Médaille de Mexique
50 Italie 1859
51 Mentana 1867
52 1870–71
53 Chine-Tonkin
54 Madagascar
55 Dahomey
56 Soudan
57 Médaille Coloniale
58 Maroc
59 Commémorative 1914–18
60 Blessés
61 Blessés Civils
62 Médaille Interalliée 1914–18
63 Victimes de l'Invasion
64 Fidélité Française
65 Prisonniers Civils
66 Haute-Silésie
67 Syrie-Cilicie
68 Orient
69 Dardanelles
70 Liban
71 Commémorative 1939–45
72 France Libre
73 Campagne d'Italie
74 Médaille de la France libérée
75 Patriotes Proscrits

PLATE 9

REPUBLIC OF FRANCE

PLATE 10

REPUBLIC OF FRANCE

MEDALS OF HONOUR

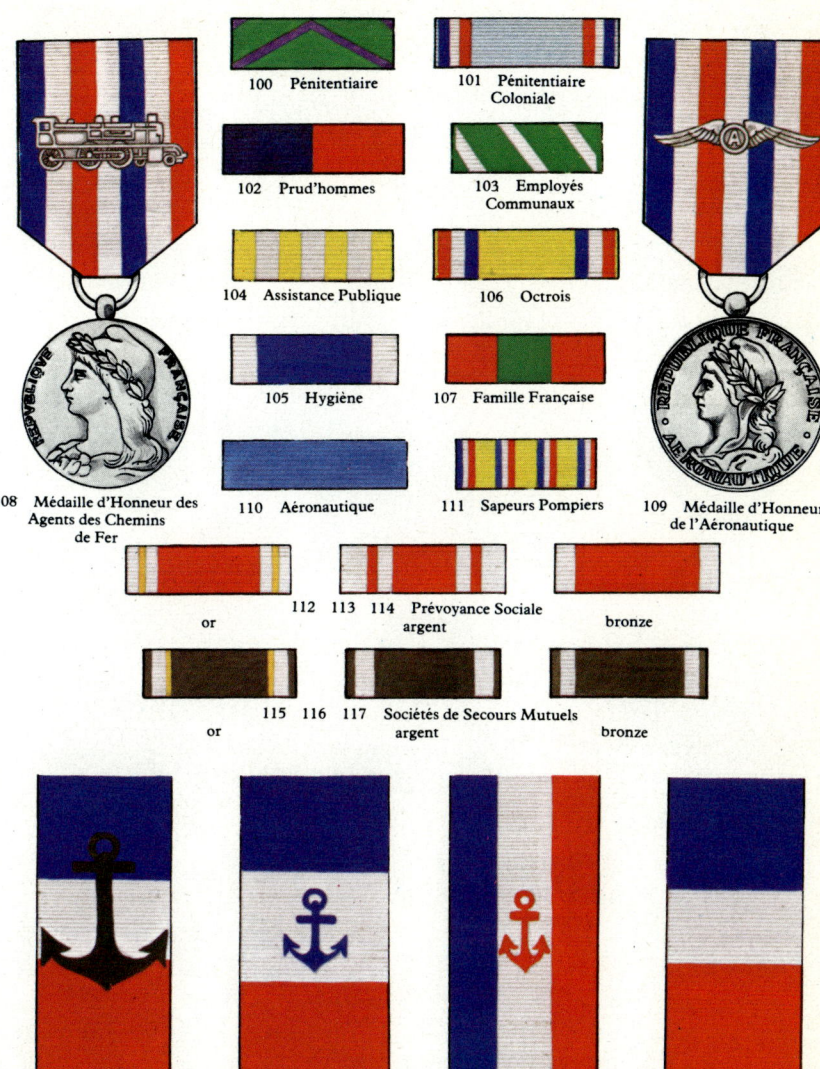

100 Pénitentiaire
101 Pénitentiaire Coloniale
102 Prud'hommes
103 Employés Communaux
104 Assistance Publique
106 Octrois
105 Hygiène
107 Famille Française
108 Médaille d'Honneur des Agents des Chemins de Fer
110 Aéronautique
111 Sapeurs Pompiers
109 Médaille d'Honneur de l'Aéronautique
112 or 113 argent 114 Prévoyance Sociale bronze
115 or 116 argent 117 Sociétés de Secours Mutuels bronze
118 Personnel non militaire de la Marine
119 Marins du Commerce
120 Courage et dévouement, Sauvetage de la Marine
121 Travail, Agricole, F.O.M.

PLATE 11

REPUBLIC OF FRANCE

COLONIAL ORDERS AND DECORATIONS (AFRICA)

123 Grand Croix
124 Grand Officier
126 Officier
127 Chevalier
122 Étoile Noire du Bénin
125 Commandeur
128 Nichan El Anouar Officier
129 Étoile d'Anjouan
130 Ordre de l'Étoile de Comore – Chevalier
131 Nichan Iftikhar
132 Ahed El Aman
133 Mérite Hafidien
134 135 Ouissam Alaouite
136 Douanes Tunisienne
137 Médaille de Dahir
138 Mérite Militaire
139 Mérite Civil
140 Police Tunisienne

PLATE 12

REPUBLIC OF FRANCE

COLONIAL ORDERS AND DECORATIONS (AFRICA AND ASIA)

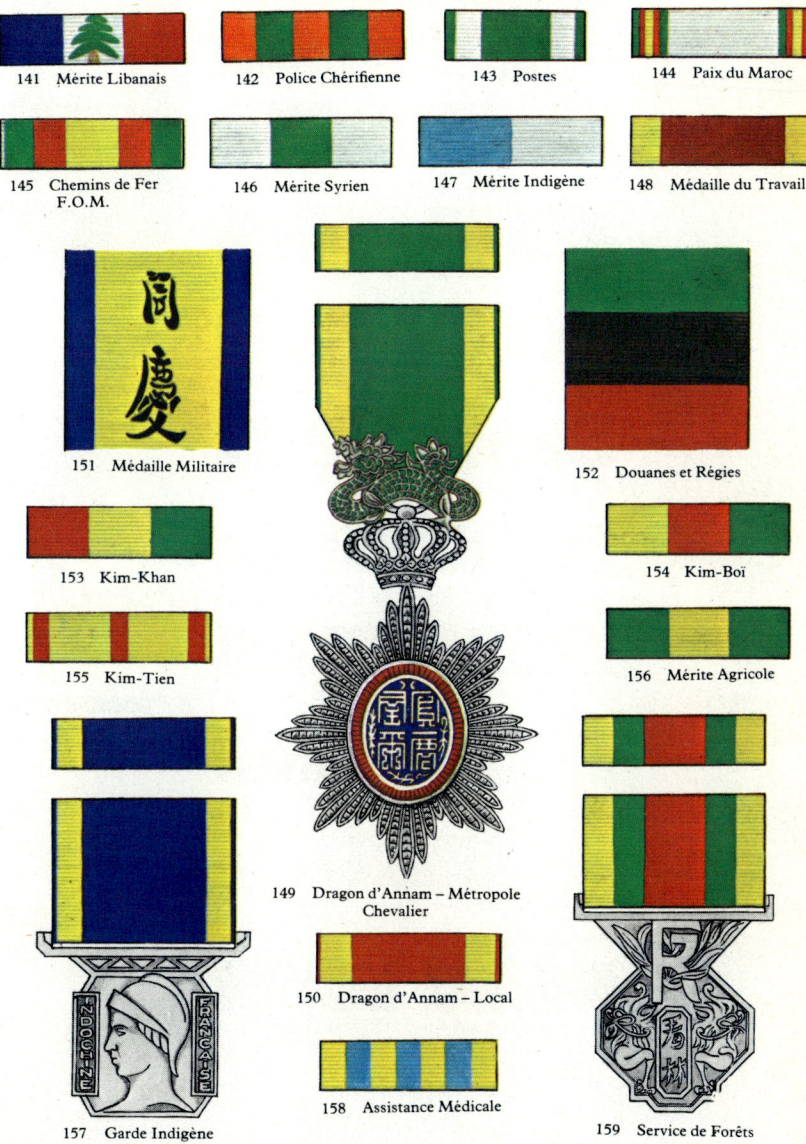

PLATE 13

REPUBLIC OF FRANCE

COLONIAL ORDERS AND DECORATIONS (ASIA)

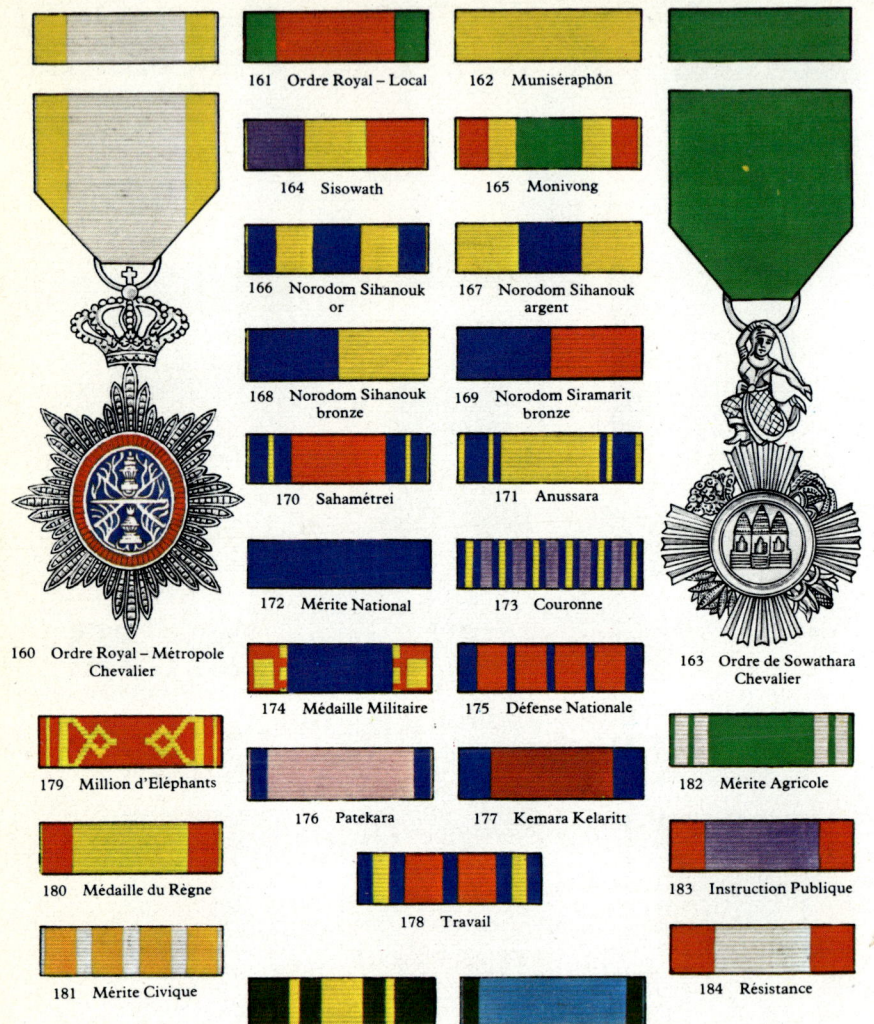

161 Ordre Royal – Local
162 Muniséraphôn
164 Sisowath
165 Monivong
166 Norodom Sihanouk or
167 Norodom Sihanouk argent
168 Norodom Sihanouk bronze
169 Norodom Siramarit bronze
170 Sahamétrei
171 Anussara
172 Mérite National
173 Couronne
160 Ordre Royal – Métropole Chevalier
163 Ordre de Sowathara Chevalier
174 Médaille Militaire
175 Défense Nationale
179 Million d'Eléphants
176 Patekara
177 Kemara Kelaritt
182 Mérite Agricole
180 Médaille du Règne
183 Instruction Publique
181 Mérite Civique
178 Travail
184 Résistance
185 Mérite Civil
186 Mérite Militaire

PLATE 14

GERMANY—EMPIRE

ORDERS, DECORATIONS AND MEDALS

2 Ehrenkreuz des Weltkrieges 1914–18 für Frontkämpfer

3 Ehrenkreuz des Weltkrieges 1914–18 für die Witwen und Eltern gefallener Kriegsteilnehmer

5 Eisernes Kreuz für Kombattanten

1 Orden Pour le Mérite

6 Eisernes Kreuz für Nicht-Kombattanten

7 German ribbons' bar – old type

8 Bandspange 1914 zum Eisernen Kreuz 1870

9 Kaiser-Wilhelm-Erinnerungsmedaille

10 China-Denkmünze

11 Südwestafrika-Denkmünze

12 Kolonial-Denkmünze

4 Eisernes Kreuz 1. Klasse

13 Schlesisches Bewährungsabzeichen (Schlesischer Adler) 2. Stufe

14 Bremisches Hanseatenkreuz

15 Lübeckisches Hanseatenkreuz

16 Hamburgisches Hanseatenkreuz

17 Baltenkreuz

GERMANY
THIRD REICH

ORDERS AND DECORATIONS

19 Verdienstorden vom Deutschen Adler
20 Verdienstorden von Deutschen Adler mit Schwertern
21 Spange 1939 zum E.K. 2. Klasse 1914
26 Kriegsverdienstkreuz 2. Klasse mit Schwertern
23 Eisernes Kreuz 2. Klasse
18 Grosskreuz des Deutschen Adlerordens
27 Kriegsverdienstmedaille
22 Eisernes Kreuz 2. Klasse
25 Kriegsverdienstkreuz 2. Klasse mit Schwertern
28 Deutsches Rotes Kreuz Volkspflege
24 Deutscher Orden
29 Deutsches Olympia-Ehrenzeichen 2. Klasse

PLATE 16

GERMANY
THIRD REICH

DECORATIONS AND MEDALS

32 Rettungsmedaille

30 Deutsches Kreuz in Silber

33 Luftschutz-Ehrenzeichen

34 Feuerwehr-Ehrenzeichen

35 Grubenwehr-Ehrenzeichen

36 Deutsches Schutzwall-Ehrenzeichen

37 Ehrenkreuz für Hinterbliebene deutscher Spanienkämpfer

38 Medaille zur Erinnerung an den 13. März 1938

39 Med. zur Erinnerung an den 1 Oktober 1938 Spange 'Prager Burg'

40

41 Med. zur Erinnerung an die Heimkehr des Memellandes

Med. 'Winterschlacht im Osten 1941–42'

42 Feldzug in Afrika

43 Tapferkeits- und Erinnerungsmedaille der Spanischen 'Blauen Division'

44 Mussert-Kreuz

45 Azad Hind

46 für Verdienste 2. Klasse in Gold

47 für Tapferkeit 2. Klasse in Silber

31 Ehrenzeichen vom 9. Nov. 1923 (Blutorden)

49 1. Stufe

50 2. Stufe

Tapferkeits- und Verdienst-Auszeichnung für Angehörige der Ostvölker

Dienstauszeichnung der NSDAP

48 für Verdienste 2. Klasse in Bronze

52 Ehrenkreuz der Deutschen Mutter

51 3. Stufe

GERMANY
THIRD REICH

LONG SERVICE AWARDS

54 55 56 Dienstauszeichnung der Wehrmacht

53 Dienstauszeichnung – Heer
1. Klasse mit Eichenlaub

57 58 SS-Dienstauszeichnung

59 Polizei
Dienstauszeichnung
60 Zollgrenzschutz-Ehrenzeichen

Treudienst-Ehrenzeichen
61 1. Stufe

63 Dienstauszeichnung
für den Reichsarbeitsdienst

62 2. Stufe

SOME RIBBONS OF THE GERMAN STATES AND OF AUSTRIA

65 Baden
Militär-Verdienstkreuz

66 Bayern
Militär-Verdienstmedaille
Tapferkeitsmedaille

67 Bayern
König Ludwigs-Kreuz

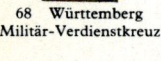
68 Württemberg
Militär-Verdienstkreuz

69 Tiroler Landesdenkmünze
1914–18

64 Eisernes Kreuz
2. Klasse

70 Danziger Kreuz
2. Klasse

71 Österreich-Ungarn
Kriegsverdienstmedaille

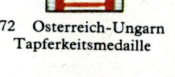
72 Osterreich-Ungarn
Tapferkeitsmedaille

73 Österreich-Ungarn
Karl-Truppenkreuz

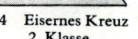
74 Kroatien
Tapferkeitsmedaille

PLATE 18

GERMANY
DEMOCRATIC REPUBLIC

ORDERS AND MEDALS

1 Karl-Marx-Orden

2 Vaterländischer Verdienstorden in Gold

3 in Silber

4 Scharnhorst-Orden

5 6 Orden 'Banner der Arbeit'

7 Kampforden für Verdienste um Volk und Vaterland

9 Verdienstmedaille der NVA

10 Medaille der Waffenbrüderschaft

11 Medaille für vorbildlichen Grenzdienst

12 Medaille für treue Dienste in der NVA

13 Friedrich-Engels-Preis

8 Stern der Völkerfreundschaft in Silber

14 Theodor-Körner-Preis

PLATE 19

GERMANY
FEDERAL REPUBLIC

ORDERS AND DECORATIONS

1 Verdienstorden der Bundesrepublik Deutschland

4 Sonderstufe des Grosskreuzes des Verdienstordens

6 Grosses Verdienstkreuz mit Stern und Schulterband

5 Grosskreuz des Verdienstordens

7 Grosses Verdienstkreuz mit Stern

8 9 Grosses Verdienstkreuz

10 Verdienstkreuz Erster Klasse

11 12 Verdienstkreuz am Bande

2 Verdienstkreuzes

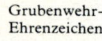

13 Verdienstmedaille

3 Verdienstmedaille

Grubenwehr-Ehrenzeichen

15 in Gold

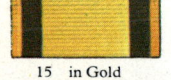

16 in Silber

19 Rettungsmedaille

14 Orden Pour le Mérite für Wissenschaften und Künste

Ehrenzeichen des Deutschen Roten Kreuzes

17 in Gold

18 in Silber

20 Deutsches Sportabzeichen
1. Klasse   2. Klasse

PLATE 20

GERMANY – FEDERAL REPUBLIC

DECORATIONS AND MEDALS

21 Ritterkreuz des Eisernes Kreuzes

22 Ehrenblattspange Heer

23 Ehrenblattspange Kriegsmarine

24 Ehrenblattspange Luftwaffe

25 Deutsches Kreuz in Gold

28 Eisernes Kreuz 1. Klasse

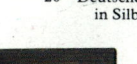
26 Deutsches Kreuz in Silber

29 Eisernes Kreuz 2. Klasse

27 Eisernes Kreuz 1. Klasse

34 Nahkampfspange Heer

31 Kriegsverdienstkreuz

32 Kriegsverdienstkreuz 2. Klasse mit Schwertern

35 Frontflugspange Jäger

36 Infanterie-Sturmabzeichen

37 Flugzeugführer- und Beobachterabzeichen

38 Panzervernichtungsabzeichen

39 Verwundetenabzeichen

40 Ärmelband 'Afrika'

30 Kriegsverdienstkreuz 1. Klasse mit Schwertern

41 Ärmelband 'Kurland'

33 Kriegsverdienstmedaille

42 18 Jahre Dienstzeit

43 4 Jahre Dienstzeit

PLATE 21

GREAT BRITAIN

VICTORIA AND GEORGE CROSS, AND ORDERS OF KNIGHTHOOD

1. Victoria Cross
2. Victoria Cross Navy 1856
3. Victoria Cross Army 1856
4. George Cross
5. The Most Noble Order of the Garter
6. The Most Noble and Most Ancient Order of the Thistle
7. The Most Illustrious Order of St. Patrick
8. Order of the Bath
9. Order of Merit
10. Order of the Star of India
11. Order of St. Michael and St. George
12. Order of the Indian Empire
13. Royal Victorian Order
14. Order of the Companions of Honour
15. Royal Guelphic Order
16. Distinguished Service Order

PLATE 22

GREAT BRITAIN

ORDERS AND DECORATIONS

17 Order of the British Empire
Civil – 1917-36

18 Order of the British Empire
Military – 1917-36

22 Imperial Service Order
and Medal

24 Order of British India
1st Class – 2nd type

25 Order of British India
2nd Class – 2nd type

28 Indian Order of Merit
Military

31 Kaiser-I-Hind Medal

19 Order of the British Empire
Badge

20 Order of the British Empire
Civil – post-1936

21 Order of the British Empire
Military – post-1936

23 Order of British India
1st type

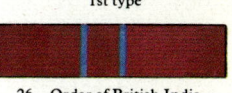
26 Order of British India
1st Class – 3rd type

27 Order of British India
2nd Class – 3rd type

29 Indian Order of Merit
Civil

32 Order of Burma

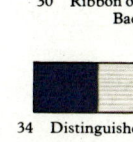
30 Ribbon of the Baronet's
Badge

33 Royal Red Cross

34 Distinguished Service Cross

35 Military Cross

36 Navy Conspicuous
Gallantry Medal – 1st type

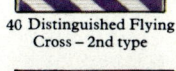
38 Distinguished Flying
Cross – 1st type

39 Air Force Cross
1st type

42 R.A.F. Conspicuous
Gallantry Medal

37 Navy Conspicuous
Gallantry Medal – 2nd type

40 Distinguished Flying
Cross – 2nd type

41 Air Force Cross
2nd type

43 Burma Gallantry
Medal

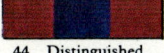
44 Distinguished
Conduct Medal

45 R.W.A.F.F./K.A.R.
D.C.M

46 Navy Distinguished
Service Medal

47 Indian D.S.M.

PLATE 23

GREAT BRITAIN

ORDERS, DECORATIONS AND MEDALS

48 George Medal

57 Order of St. John of Jerusalem

49 Edward Medal

50 Military Medal

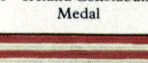
51 Ireland Constabulary Medal

52 Distinguished Flying Medal 1st type

54 Air Force Medal 1st type

53 Distinguished Flying Medal 2nd type

55 Air Force Medal 2nd type

60 British Empire Medal Civil – 1st type

56 Order of St. John of Jerusalem Knight of Grace's Breast Star

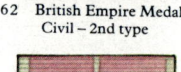
62 British Empire Medal Civil – 2nd type

61 British Empire Medal Military – 1st type

58 St. John Life Saving Medal

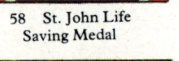
59 St. John Service Medal

63 British Empire Medal Military – 2nd type

64 Queen's Police D.S.M.

66 Queen's Fire Service D.S.M.

68 India Police D.C.M.

65 Queen's Police Gallantry Medal

67 Queen's Fire Service Gallantry Medal

69 India Police Gallantry Medal

70 Special Constabulary Faithful Service Medal

72 Hong Kong Police Medal 1st Class

73 Hong Kong Police Medal 2nd Class

71 Sudan Defence Force D.C.M.

74 Hong Kong Police Medal 3rd Class

75 Hong Kong Police Medal 4th Class

76 Union of South Africa Queen's Medal for Bravery

77 Sarawak Consp. Bravery Medal

78 Canadian Forces Decoration

79 Polar Medals

PLATE 24

GREAT BRITAIN

WAR MEDALS

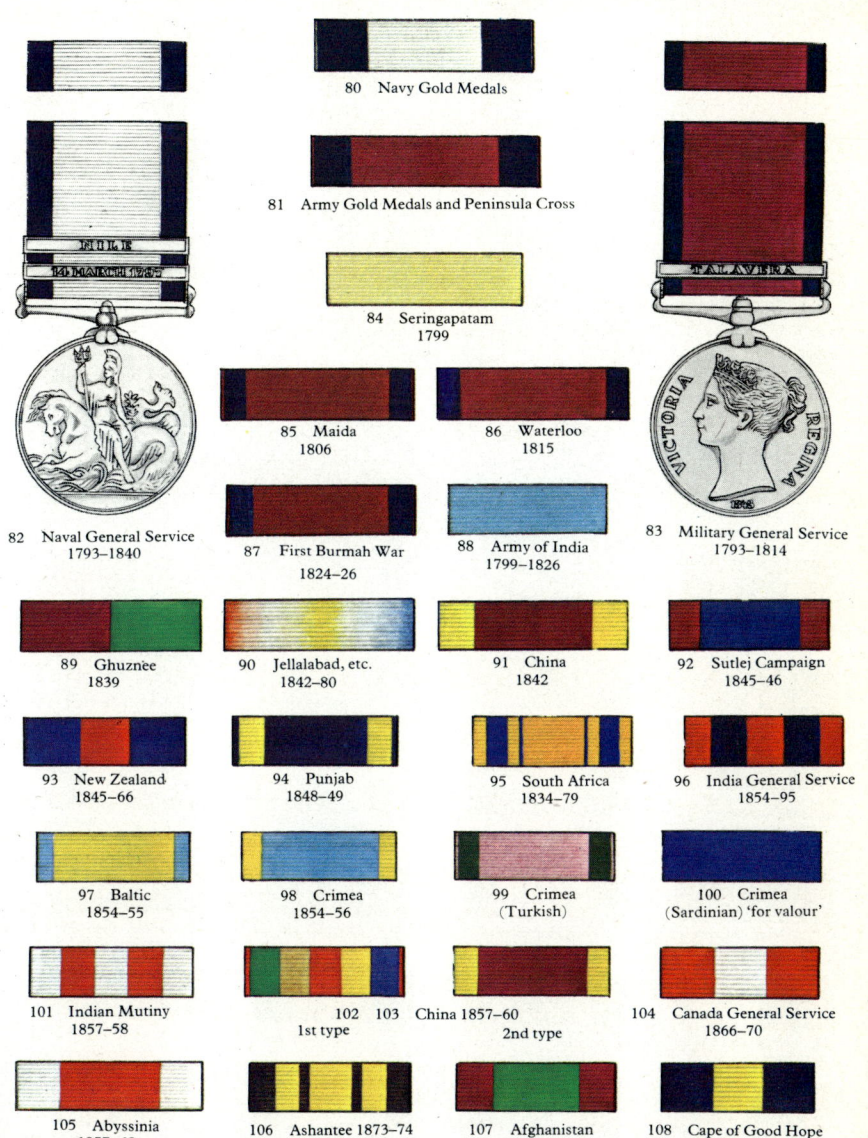

80 Navy Gold Medals

81 Army Gold Medals and Peninsula Cross

84 Seringapatam 1799

85 Maida 1806

86 Waterloo 1815

82 Naval General Service 1793–1840

87 First Burmah War 1824–26

88 Army of India 1799–1826

83 Military General Service 1793–1814

89 Ghuznee 1839

90 Jellalabad, etc. 1842–80

91 China 1842

92 Sutlej Campaign 1845–46

93 New Zealand 1845–66

94 Punjab 1848–49

95 South Africa 1834–79

96 India General Service 1854–95

97 Baltic 1854–55

98 Crimea 1854–56

99 Crimea (Turkish)

100 Crimea (Sardinian) 'for valour'

101 Indian Mutiny 1857–58

102 103 China 1857–60
1st type   2nd type

104 Canada General Service 1866–70

105 Abyssinia 1857–68

106 Ashantee 1873–74
East/West Africa 1887–1900

107 Afghanistan 1878–80

108 Cape of Good Hope 1880–97

PLATE 25

GREAT BRITAIN

WAR MEDALS

PLATE 26

GREAT BRITAIN

WAR MEDALS

143 British War Medal 1914–20
144 Territorial Force War Medal 1914–19
145 Mercantile Marine Medal 1914–18
146 Gallipoli Star (not issued)
147 General Service 1918–64
148 W.W.1 Victory Medal
149 India General Service 1936
150 Sudan Defence Force General Service
151 1939–1945 Star
155 France and Germany Star
156 Atlantic Star
157 Pacific Star
158 Italy Star
159 Burma Star
160 Defence Medal
161 War Medal 1939–45
162 Canada Medal
152 Africa Star 1st Army
153 Eighth Army
154 Air Crew Europe Star
163 Canada Volunteer Service Medal
164 Australia Service Medal 1939–45
165 New Zealand War Service Medal 1939–45
166 South Africa Africa Service Medal
167 South Africa War Service Medal
168 Southern Rhodesia W.W.2 Service Medal
169 India General Service 1939–45
170 India Independence Medal
171 India Police Independence Medal
172 Pakistan Independence
173 Korea 1950–53
174 U.N. Korea
175 U.N. Cyprus
176 Malaya Independence
177 General Service 1962
178 Vietnam Medal Australia

PLATE 27

GREAT BRITAIN

CORONATION, JUBILEE MEDALS, ROYAL HOUSEHOLD RIBBONS, ETC.

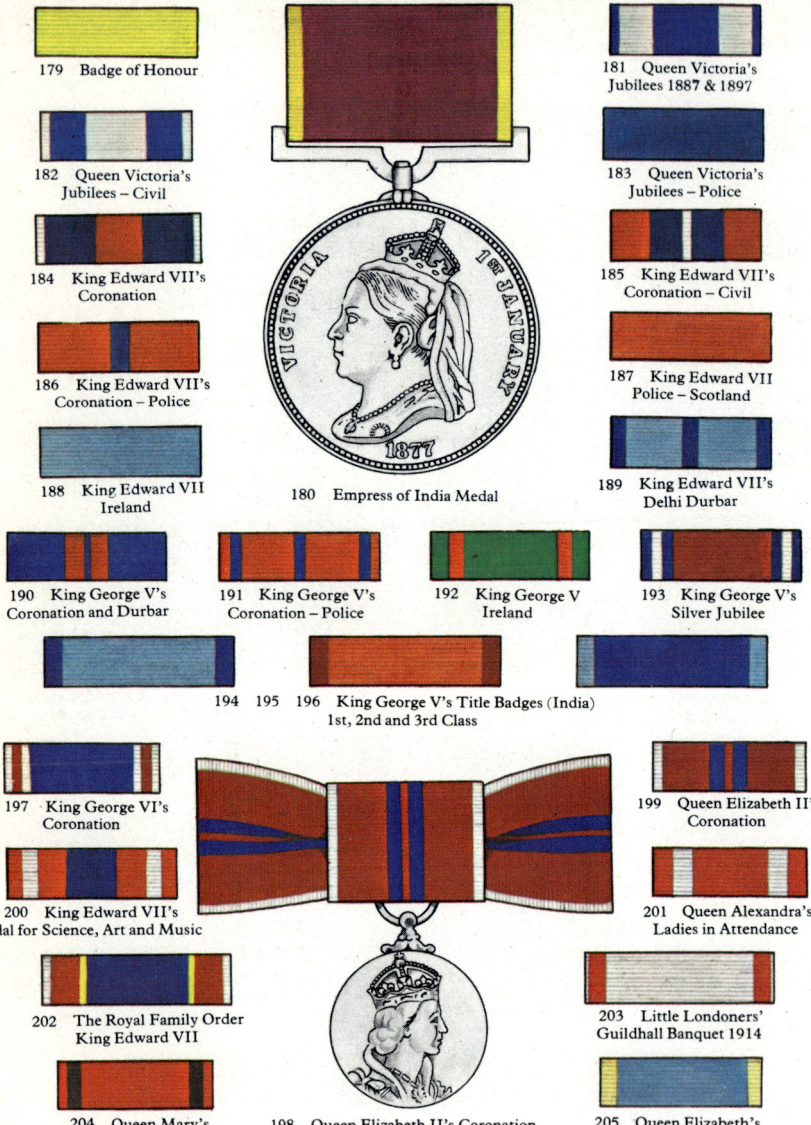

179 Badge of Honour
180 Empress of India Medal
181 Queen Victoria's Jubilees 1887 & 1897
182 Queen Victoria's Jubilees – Civil
183 Queen Victoria's Jubilees – Police
184 King Edward VII's Coronation
185 King Edward VII's Coronation – Civil
186 King Edward VII's Coronation – Police
187 King Edward VII Police – Scotland
188 King Edward VII Ireland
189 King Edward VII's Delhi Durbar
190 King George V's Coronation and Durbar
191 King George V's Coronation – Police
192 King George V Ireland
193 King George V's Silver Jubilee
194 195 196 King George V's Title Badges (India) 1st, 2nd and 3rd Class
197 King George VI's Coronation
198 Queen Elizabeth II's Coronation Medal worn by Ladies
199 Queen Elizabeth II's Coronation
200 King Edward VII's Medal for Science, Art and Music
201 Queen Alexandra's Ladies in Attendance
202 The Royal Family Order King Edward VII
203 Little Londoners' Guildhall Banquet 1914
204 Queen Mary's Ladies in Attendance
205 Queen Elizabeth's Ladies in Attendance

PLATE 28

GREAT BRITAIN

MERITORIOUS SERVICE, LONG SERVICE AND GOOD CONDUCT MEDALS AND TERRITORIAL DECORATIONS

GREAT BRITAIN

MERITORIOUS SERVICE, LONG SERVICE AND GOOD CONDUCT MEDALS

241 R.W.A.F.F./K.A.R. L.S. & G.C. Medal

242 Permanent Overseas Forces L.S. & G.C.M.

243 Canada L.S. & G.C.M.

244 Australia M.S. Medal

245 Union of South Africa M.S. Medal

246 Cape of Good Hope L.S. & G.C.M.

247 Australia L.S. & G.C.M.

248 Victoria Long and Efficient S.M.

249 Sarawak L.S. Medal

250 New Guinea L.S. & G.C.M.

251 New Zealand L.S. & G.C.M.

252 New Zealand Long and Efficient Service

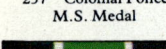
253 Police L.S. & G.C.M.

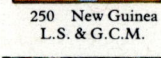
254 Colonial Police Gallantry Medal

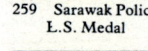
255 R. Canadian Mounted Police L.S. & G.C.M.

256 Fire Brigade L.S. & G.C.M.

257 Colonial Police M.S. Medal

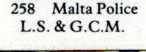
258 Malta Police L.S. & G.C.M.

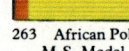
259 Sarawak Police L.S. Medal

260 Colonial Fire Brigade L.S. Medal

261 Colonial Police L.S. Medal

262 Ceylon Police L.S. & G.C.M.

263 African Police M.S. Medal

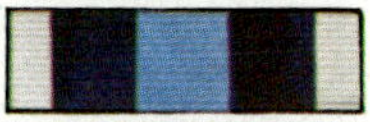

264 Burma Police M.S. Medal

ROYAL HOUSEHOLD LONG AND FAITHFUL SERVICE MEDALS

265 Queen Victoria's Faithful Service Medal

266 King George V (obsolete type)

267 King George V

268 King George VI

269 Queen Elizabeth II

270 Queen Elizabeth II's L. & F. Service Medal

GOOD SHOOTING MEDALS, ETC.

271 Army Best Shot

272 R.A.F. Best Shot

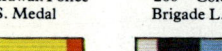
273 Royal Observer Corps Medal

274 Indian Army Best Shot

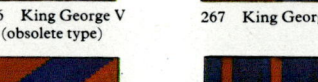
275 National Rifle Association

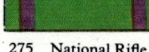
276 Cadet Forces Medal

PLATE 30

GREAT BRITAIN

OTHER MEDALS

PLATE 31

PEOPLE'S REPUBLIC OF HUNGARY

ORDERS, DECORATIONS AND MEDALS (Modern)

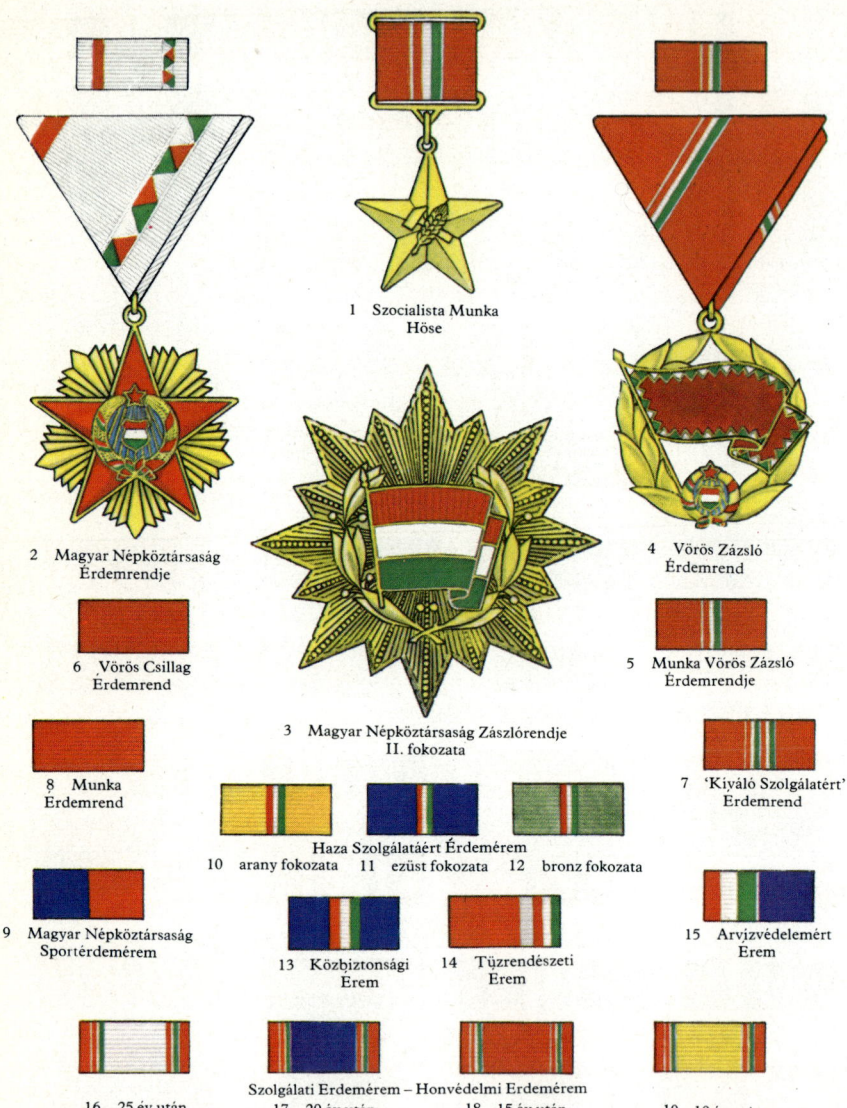

1 Szocialista Munka Hőse
2 Magyar Népköztársaság Érdemrendje
3 Magyar Népköztársaság Zászlórendje II. fokozata
4 Vörös Zázsló Érdemrend
5 Munka Vörös Zázsló Érdemrendje
6 Vörös Csillag Erdemrend
7 'Kiváló Szolgálatért' Erdemrend
8 Munka Erdemrend
9 Magyar Népköztársaság Sportérdemérem
Haza Szolgálatért Érdemérem
10 arany fokozata 11 ezüst fokozata 12 bronz fokozata
13 Közbiztonsági Erem
14 Tüzrendészeti Erem
15 Arvízvédelemért Erem
Szolgálati Érdemérem – Honvédelmi Érdemérem
16 25 év után 800 repült óra után
17 20 év után 550 repült óra után
18 15 év után 350 repült óra után
19 10 év után 200 repült óra után

PLATE 32

PEOPLE'S REPUBLIC OF HUNGARY

ORDERS, DECORATIONS AND MEDALS (Obsolete)

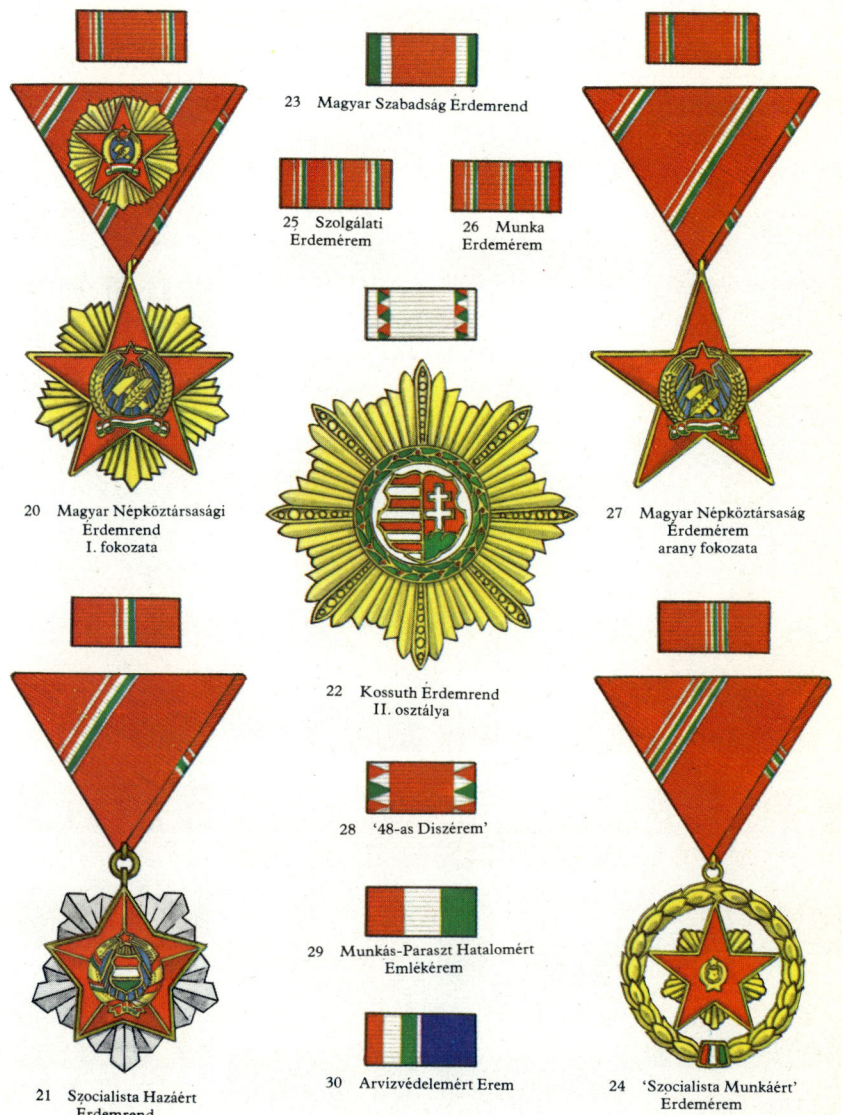

20 Magyar Népköztársasági Érdemrend I. fokozata
23 Magyar Szabadság Érdemrend
25 Szolgálati Érdemérem
26 Munka Érdemérem
27 Magyar Népköztársaság Érdemérem arany fokozata
22 Kossuth Érdemrend II. osztálya
28 '48-as Díszérem'
29 Munkás-Paraszt Hatalomért Emlékérem
21 Szocialista Hazáért Érdemrend
30 Árvízvédelemért Érem
24 'Szocialista Munkáért' Érdemérem

PLATE 33

EMPIRE OF IRAN

ORDERS, DECORATIONS AND MEDALS

PLATE 34

KINGDOM OF ITALY

ORDERS

1 Ordine Supremo della SS. Annunziata

2 Ordine dei SS. Maurizio e Lazzaro
   Cavaliere di Gran Croce

3 Ordine Militare di Savoia
   Grande Ufficiale

4 Ordine Civile di Savoia

6 Cavaliere di Gran Croce

9 Cavaliere Ufficiale

7 Grande Ufficiale

10 Cavaliere

11 Ordine al Merito del Lavoro

14 Ordine dell'Aquila Romana

12 Stella al Merito del Lavoro
    1° tipo

15 Ordine Coloniale della Stella
    d'Italia – Cavaliere

13 Stella al Merito del Lavoro
    2° tipo

5 Ordine della Corona d'Italia
8 Commendatore

16 Unità d'Italia

ALBANIAN ORDERS

17 Ordine della Besa

18 Cavaliere di Gran Croce

Ordine di Scanderbeg

19 Grande Ufficiale

21 Cavaliere Ufficiale

20 Commendatore

22 Cavaliere

PLATE 35

KINGDOM OF ITALY

DECORATIONS

24 25 26   Medaglie al Valore Militare – oro, argento, bronzo

27 28 29   Medaglie al Valore di Marina – oro, argento, bronzo

30 31 32   Medaglie al Valore Aeronautico – oro, argento, bronzo

33 34 35   Medaglie al Valore Civile – oro, argento, bronzo

23 Medaglia d'oro al Valore Militare

37 Croce al Merito di Guerra   38 2ª concessione

 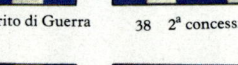

39 5ª concessione   40 8ª concessione

41 Croce di Guerra al Valore Militare

42 Croce d'Oriente Macedonia   43 Croce di Guerra Fascista

45 Croce della campagna di Spagna   46 Croce di Guerra Ferroviaria

36 Croce di Guerra

47 Valore al Campo (non addottata)

44 Croce della campagna di Spagna

PLATE 36

KINGDOM OF ITALY

WAR MEDALS

48 Crimea

49 Campagna 1859

50 Spedizione dei Mille

51 Campagna 1870

52 Guerre di Indipendenza

53 Eritrea 1891–96

54 Cina 1900–01

55 Guerra Italo-turca 1911 Libia

59 Guerra 1915–18

57 Volontario di Guerra 1915–1918

60 Volontario Irredento

61 Vittoria Interalleata

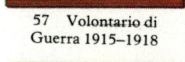
62 Fiume

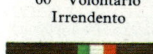
63 Campagna Fascista

64 Marcia su Roma

65 Campagna d'Etiopia 1935–36

66 Campagna di Etiopia – Fronte Sud

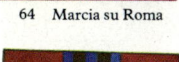
67 Volontario in A.O.I.

68 Impero

58 Medaglia della Guerra 1915–18

69 Legionario Italiano in Spagna

70 71 Volontario in Spagna 2 tipi

72

73 74 Campagna di Spagna 3 tipi

75 Campagna di Spagna 4° tipo

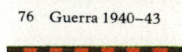
76 Guerra 1940–43

77 Volontario di Guerra 1940–43

78 Campagna di Francia

79 Campagna d'Albania

80 Corpo di Spedizione Italiano in Russia

81 Campagna d'Africa (italo-tedesca)

82 Servizio per la Repubblica Sociale Italiana

83 Campagna di Liberazione

56 Medaglia di Volontario di Guerra

PLATE 37

KINGDOM OF ITALY

LONG SERVICE AWARDS

84 10 lustri di servizio militare (Mauriziana)

85 Lungo Comando Regio Esercito

86 Lungo Comando Guardia di Finanza

87 88 89 Lunga Navigazione Marittima
20 anni   15 anni   10 anni

90 91 92 Lunga Navigazione Aerea
20 anni   15 anni   10 anni

SENIORITY AWARDS

94 Croce di Anzianità M.V.S.N.

93 Anzianità Servizio Regio Esercito

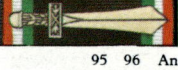
95 96 Anzianità M.V.S.N.
10 anni   20 anni

97 Anzianità Pubblica Sicurezza

98 Anzianità Polizia Africa Italiana

99 Anzianità Guardia di Finanza

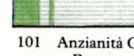
100 Anzianita Vigili del Fuoco

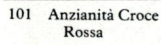
101 Anzianità Croce Rossa

COMMEMORATIVE MEDALS AND CROSSES OF MILITARY FORMATIONS

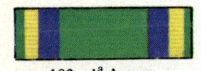
102 1ᵃ Armata

103 2ᵃ Armata

104 3ᵃ Armata

105 4ᵃ Armata

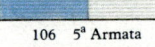
106 5ᵃ Armata

107 6ᵃ Armata

108 7ᵃ Armata

109 8ᵃ, 9ᵃ, 10ᵃ Armata

111 11ᵃ Armata

110 Croce dell' 11ᵃ Armata

112 Divisione '28 Marzo'

113 Divisione 'Tevere'

114 Divisione 'Freccie Nere'

PLATE 38

KINGDOM OF ITALY

MEDALS OF MERIT AND OTHER AWARDS

115 Merito di Servizio Truppe Indigene

116 Benemeriti Educazione Popolare

117 Ben. Istruzione, Cultura dell'Arte

118 Stella al Merito della Scuola

119 Benemeriti Salute Pubblica

120 Merito Sanità Pubblica

121 Servizi Pubblici

123 Madri e vedove dei caduti

124 Benemeriti Croce Rossa

125 Merito Croce Rossa

126 Merito Agrario e Industriale (1898)

127 Stella al Merito Rurale

129 Merito Agricolo, Commerciale e Industriale (A.O.I.)

130 Benemeriti Terremoto Calabro-Siculo

131 Commemorativa Terr. Calabro-Siculo

132 Terremoto della Marsica

133 Lavoratori in A.O.I.

134 Merito Redenzione Sociale

135 Madri Prolifiche

122 Medaglia per le madri e vedove dei caduti

136 Merito di Servizio Vigili del Fuoco

137 Scuole Italiane all'Estero

138 Mostra Rivoluzione Fascista

139 Nazionalisti

140 Veterani al Pantheon

141 Tiro a Segno Nazionale

142 Pionieri della Aeronautica

143 Crociera Decennale

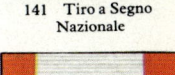 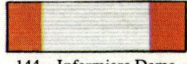
144 Infermiere Dame Croce Rossa

145 Ministero degli Esteri

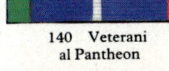
146 Cappellano Militare

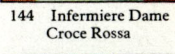
147 Cinquantenario Alpini

128 Medaglia al Merito Agricolo, Commerciale e Industriale (A.O.I.)

148 Commemorativa dell'Asse

149 Commemorativa del Tripartito

PLATE 39

KINGDOM OF ITALY

FASCIST, ATHLETIC AND OTHER AWARDS

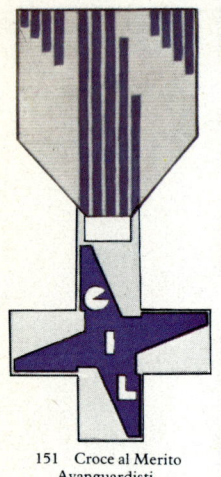

151 Croce al Merito Avanguardisti

150 Merito Giovani Fascisti

152 Merito Avanguardisti

153 Merito Giovani Italiane

154 Merito Balilla

155 Merito Piccole Italiane

156 Capo Centuria Campeggio 'Dux'

157 Campeggio 'Dux'

158 Valore Atletico oro

159 Valore Atletico argento 1 grado

160 Valore Atletico argento

161 Valore Atletico bronzo

162 Stella al Merito Sportivo

163 Benemeriti G.I.L.

164 Benemeriti O.N.D.

ITALIAN REPUBLIC

ORDERS, DECORATIONS AND MEDALS

2 Cavaliere di Gran Croce

3 Grande Ufficiale Ordine Militare d'Italia

4 Commendatore

5 Cavaliere Ufficiale

6 Cavaliere

7 Ordine dei SS. Maurizio e Lazzaro – Grande Ufficiale

8 Ordine della Corona d'Italia – Commendatore

9 Ordine Coloniale della Stella d'Italia – Cavaliere

10 Ordine al Merito del Lavoro

11 Stella al Merito del Lavoro

12 Volontari della Libertà

1 Ordine Militare d'Italia Cavaliere

PLATE 40

ITALIAN REPUBLIC

ORDERS, DECORATIONS AND MEDALS

14 Cavaliere di Gran Croce

15 Grande Ufficiale

16 Commendatore

13 Ordine al Merito della Repubblica

17 Cavaliere Ufficiale

18 Cavaliere

19 Ordine della Stella della Solidarietà Italiana

20 Ordine di Vittorio Veneto

21 Viaggi di Stato del Presidente della Repubblica

22 Anzianità Servizio 25 anni

23 Lungo Comando Esercito 20 anni

24 Anzianità Guardia di Finanza – 40 anni

25 Lungo Comando Guardia di Finanza – 20 anni

Commenda

27 Lungo Comando Pubblica Sicurezza – 15 anni

26 Lunga Navigazione Aerea 15 anni

MEDALS FOR VALOUR

28 29 30 Al Valore Militare – oro, argento, bronzo

OTHERS

40 Croce al Merito di Guerra 2ª concessione

31 32 33 Al Valore di Marina – oro, argento, bronzo

41 Croce di Guerra al Valore Militare

34 35 36 Al Valore Aeronautico – oro, argento, bronzo

42 Medaglia al Merito Civile – argento

37 38 39 Al Valore Civile – oro, argento, bronzo

43 Benemeriti Istruzione, Cultura dell'arte

KINGDOM OF THE NETHERLANDS

ORDERS, DECORATIONS AND MEDALS

2 Orde van de Nederlandse Leeuw

3 Orde van Oranje-Nassau

4 Eremedaille Oranje-Nassau

5 Bronzen Leeuw

7 Bronzen Kruis

9 Vliegerkruis

1 Militaire Willemsorde

11 Ereteken voor belangrijke krijgsverrichtingen

6 Verzetsster Oost-Azië 1942–45

8 Kruis van Verdienste

10 Erepenning voor menslievend hulpbetoon

12 Oorlogs-Herinneringskruis

13 Ereteken voor Orde en Vrede

14 Herinneringskruis Nieuw-Guinea

15 Mobilisatie-Oorlogskruis

16 Kruis voor Recht en Vrijheid – Korea

17 Onderscheidingsteken voor langdurige dienst als officier

18 Onderscheidingsteken voor langdurige dienst als onderofficier

19 Vrijwilligers-medaille

20 Huwelijksmedaille 1937

21 Inhuldigingsmedaille 1948

22 Medaille van het Rote Kruis

23 Marsvaardigheid

24 Medaille van het Nederlands Olympisch Comité

25 Militaire Vijfkamp Kruis

26 Mobilisatiekruis 1914–18

PLATE 42

KINGDOM OF NORWAY

ORDERS, DECORATIONS AND MEDALS

3 Krigskorset
5 St. Olavsmedaljen
8 Krigsmedaljen
10 Den Norske Koreamedalje
4 Medaljen for edel dåd
7 Haakon VII's Frihetskors
9 Deltakermedaljen 1940–45
11 Haakon VII's Frihetsmedalje
1 St. Olavs-orden
12 Haakon VII's 70-års medalje
13 Kongens fortjenstmedalje
14 Kroningsmedaljen
15 Borgerdådsmedaljen
16 Haakon VII's jubileumsmedalje
17 Kongens erindringsmedalje
2 Krigskorset (med ett eller flere sverd)
18 Skittermerke i gull
19 Hederstegn for Röte Kors
6 Haakon VII's Frihetskors

PLATE 43

REPUBLIC OF POLAND

ORDERS, DECORATIONS AND MEDALS

PLATE 44

REPUBLIC OF POLAND

ORDERS, DECORATIONS AND MEDALS

27 Brązowy Krzyż Zasługi

28 Medal Wojska

29 Medal Morski (Marynarki Wojennej)

30 Medal Lotniczy

31 Medal Morski (Marynarki Handlowej)

32 Krzyż Zasługi Wojsk Litwy Środkowej

33 Krzyz na Śląskiej Wstędze Waleczności Zasługi

34 Medal za Ratowanie Ginących

35 Medal Pamiątkowy za Wojnę 1918–21

36 Medal Dziesięciolecia Odzyskanej Niepodległości

37 Medal 3 Maja

38 Złoty Medal za Długoletnią Służbę (XXX lat)

39 Srebrny Medal za Długoletnią Służbę (XX lat)

40 Brązowy Medal za Długoletnią Służbę (X lat)

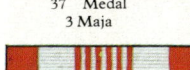
41 Krzyż Armii Krajowej

42 Odznaka Pamiątkowa 'Krzyż Pamiątkowy Monte Cassino'

43 Odznaka Honorowa za Rany i Kontuzje

POLISH PEOPLE'S REPUBLIC

ORDERS

2 Order Budowniczych Polski Ludowj

4 Order Virtuti Militari – I klasy

6 Order Sztandaru Pracy – I klasy

8 Order Virtuti Militari – II klasy

10 Order Sztandaru Pracy – II klasy

1 Order Budowniczych Polski Ludowej

3 Order Odrodzenia Polski – I klasy

5 Order Krzyża Grunwaldu – I klasy

7 Order Odrodzenia Polski – II klasy

9 Order Krzyża Grunwaldu – II klasy

11 Order Odrodzenia Polski – III klasy

PLATE 45

POLISH PEOPLE'S REPUBLIC

ORDERS, DECORATIONS AND MEDALS

12 Order Krzyża Grunwaldu – III klasy

13 Order Virtuti Militari – III klasy

14 Order Odrodzenia Polski – IV klasy

15 Order Virtuti Militari – IV klasy

16 Order Odrodzenia Polski – V klasy

17 Order Virtuti Militari – V klasy

18 Złoty Krzyż Zasługi

19 Krzyż Walecznych

20 Złoty Medal 'Zasłużonym na Polu Chwały'

21 Krzyż Partyzancki

22 Medal 'Za waszą wolność i naszą'

23 Śląski Krzyż Powstańczy

25 Wielkopolski Krzyż Powstańczy

24 Śląski Krzyż Powstańczy

26 Wielkopolski Krzyż Powstańczy

27 Srebrny Krzyż Zasługi

28 Srebrny Medal 'Zasłużonym na Polu Chwały'

29 Brązowy Krzyż Zasługi

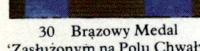
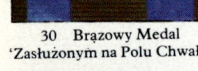

30 Brązowy Medal 'Zasłużonym na Polu Chwały'

31 'Medal za Warszawę 1939–45'

32 'Medal za Odrę, Nysę, Bałtyk'

33 'Medal Zwycięstwa i Wolności 1945'

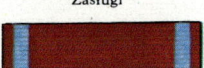

34 Medal 'Za ofiarność i Odwagę'

35 Złoty Medal 'Siły Zbrojne w Służbie Ojczyzny'

36 Srebrny Medal 'Siły Zbrojne w Służbie Ojczyzny'

38 Medal 10 lecia Polski Ludowej

37 Brązowy Medal 'Siły Zbrojne w Służbie Ojczyzny'

POLISH PEOPLE'S REPUBLIC

ORDERS AND MEDALS

40 Medal 'Za długoletnie pożycie małżeńskie'
41 Medal 'Za udział w walkach o Berlin'
42 Złoty Medal 'Za zasługi dla obronności kraju'
43 Srebrny Medal 'Za zasługi dla obronności kraju'
44 Brązowy Medal 'Za zasługi dla obronności kraju'
45 Odznaka 'Zasłużony działacz K.M.W.'
46 Złota Odznaka im. Janka Krasickiego
47 Złota Honorowa Odznaka P.C.K.
48 Złoty Medal 'Za zasługi dla pożarnictwa'
49 Złota Odznaka 'Za zasługi w zwalczaniu powodzi'
50 Srebrna Odznaka im. Janka Krasickiego
51 Srebrna Honorowa Odznaka P.C.K.
52 Srebrny Medal 'Za zasługi dla pożarnictwa'
53 Srebrna Odznaka 'Za zasługi w zwalczaniu powodzi'
54 Brązowa Odznaka im. Janka Krasickiego
55 Brązowa Honorowa Odznaka P.C.K.
56 Brązowy Medal 'Za zasługi dla pożarnictwa'
57 Brązowa Odznaka 'Za zasługi w zwalczaniu powodzi'
34 Medal 'Za ofiarność i Odwagę'
39 Medal 'Za długoletnie pożycie małżeńskie'
58 Gwiazda i wielka wstęga Orderu Virtuti Militari I klasa

PLATE 47

IMPERIAL RUSSIA

ORDERS, DECORATIONS AND MEDALS

2 Order of Saint Andrew
3 Order of Saint Catherine
4 Order of Saint Alexander-Nevsky
5 Order of Saint George
7 Order of Saint Vladimir
8 Order of Saint Anne
1 Order of St. Andrew Badge
9 Order of Saint Stanislav
10 Order of the White Eagle
11 Order of Merit in Agriculture
12 St. Andrew/St. George
13 Census 1896
14 Order of Saint Nicholas
6 Order of St. Vladimir 4th Class – Military Division

PLATE 48

U.S.S.R.

ORDERS AND DECORATIONS

1　Hero of the Soviet Union

5　Order of Victory

2　Hero of Socialist Labour

4　Order of the October Revolution

6　Order of the Red Banner

7　Order of Suvorov – Army
Star of 1st Class

11　Order of Kutuzov – Army
Star of 1st Class

8　1st Class

12　1st Class

9　2nd Class　　10　3rd Class

13　2nd Class　　14　3rd Class

3　Order of Lenin

PLATE 49

U.S.S.R.

ORDERS AND DECORATIONS

15 Order of Usjakov – Navy Star of 1st Class

16 1st Class

17 2nd Class

18 Medal of Usjakov

19 Order of Nakhimov Star of 1st Class

20 1st Class

21 2nd Class

22 Medal of Nakhimov

23 Order of Bogdan Khelnitsky

24 1st Class

25 2nd Class

26 3rd Class

29 Medal for Valour

27 Order of Alexander-Nevsky

30 Medal for Meritorious Service in Battle

28 Order of the Red Star

PLATE 50

U.S.S.R.

ORDERS AND DECORATIONS

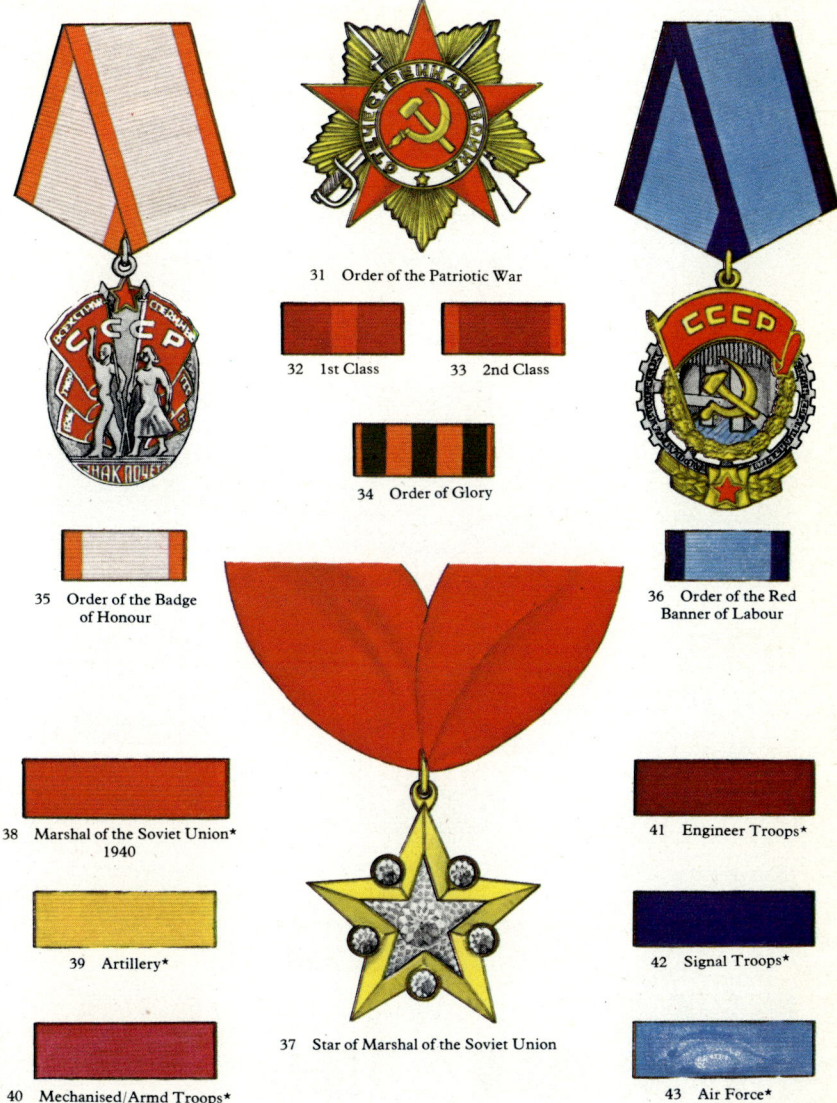

31 Order of the Patriotic War
32 1st Class
33 2nd Class
34 Order of Glory
35 Order of the Badge of Honour
36 Order of the Red Banner of Labour
37 Star of Marshal of the Soviet Union
38 Marshal of the Soviet Union* 1940
39 Artillery*
40 Mechanised/Armd Troops*
41 Engineer Troops*
42 Signal Troops*
43 Air Force*

* not worn as service ribbons

PLATE 51

U.S.S.R.

MEDALS

44 20 year Jubilee of the Red Army
 * ribbon 1938–43
45 30 year Jubilee of the Army and Navy
46 40 year Jubilee of the Soviet Armed Forces
47 50 year Jubilee of the Soviet Armed Forces
48 Silver Medal for Partisans in W.W.2
49 Bronze Medal for Partisans in W.W.2
50 Medal for Valiant Labour
51 Medal for Heroic Work during W.W.2
52 Medal for Distinguished Labour
53 Order of Glory of Motherhood
54 Defence of Leningrad
55 Defence of Odessa
56 Defence of Stalingrad
57 Defence of Sevastopol
58 Defence of Moscow
59 Defence of the Caucasus
60 Defence of the Arctic
61 Defence of Kiev
62 Victory over Germany
63 Victory over Japan

U.S.S.R.

MEDALS

64 Capture of Budapest

65 Capture of Koenigsberg

66 Capture of Vienna

69 Liberation of Belgrade

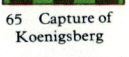
70 Liberation of Prague

71 20th Anniversary of W.W.2

72 1st Class

73 2nd Class

Good Conduct Medals

74 3rd Class

67 Capture of Berlin

68 Liberation of Warsaw

75 Centenary of Lenin

76 Restoration of Mines in Donets

77 Restoration of Heavy Industry

78 Frontier Defence Medal

79 Public Order

80 Fire Brigade

81 Reclaiming of the Virgin lands

82 Life Saving from drowning

83 800th Anniversary Foundation of Moscow

84 200th Anniversary Foundation of Leningrad

PLATE 53

U.S.A.

DECORATIONS

2   Navy Cross

4   Distinguished Service Cross
    Air Force Cross

6   Distinguished Service Medal
    Navy

8   Distinguished Service Medal
    Army

10 Distinguished Service Medal
    Coast Guard

1   Medal of Honor

3   Brevet Medal
    Marine Corps

5   Certificate of Merit

7   Distinguished Service Medal
    Merchant Marine

9   Distinguished Service Medal
    Air Force

11 Specially Meritorious Medal

12 13 14 15 Chief Commander, Commander, Officer and
             Legionnaire of the Legion of Merit

16 Silver Star

17 Soldier's Medal

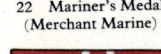
18 Distinguished Flying
    Cross

19 Airman's Medal

20 Coast Guard Medal

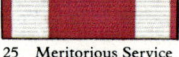
21 Navy-Marine Corps
    Medal

22 Mariner's Medal
    (Merchant Marine)

23 Bronze Star

24 Bronze Star (Valor)

25 Meritorious Service
    Medal

26 Medal for Merit
    (Civilian)

27 Air Medal

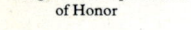
28 Congressional Space Medal
    of Honor

29 Purple Heart

30 Meritorious Service Medal
    (Merchant Marine)

31 National Security Medal

PLATE 54

U.S.A.

MEDAL OF FREEDOM, COMMENDATIONS, CITATIONS AND OTHER AWARDS

32 33 34 35 Chief Commander, Commander, Officer-Legionnaire and Medal of Freedom without palm

36 Joint Services Commendation
37 Navy Commendation
38 Army Commendation

39 Coast Guard Commendation
40 Air Force Commendation
41 Navy Achievement

42 Reserve Special Commendation
43 Presidential Unit Citation (Navy)
44 Secretary of Transportation Commendation for Achievement

45 Distinguished Civilian Service Medal
46 Navy Meritorious Unit Commendation
47 Air Force Outstanding Unit Award
48 Coast Guard Unit Commendation

49 Presidential Unit Citation (Army-A.F.)
50 Valorous Unit Award
51 Army Meritorious Unit Commendation
52 Philippine Presidential Unit Citation

53 Gallant Ship Citation (Merchant Marine)
54 Vietnam Presidential Unit Citation
55 Korean Presidential Unit Citation
56 Air Force Longevity Service Award

57 Armed Forces Reserve (10 years)
58 Naval Reserve
59 60 Marine Corps Reserve (2 types)

61 Air Reserve Forces Meritorious Service
62 Navy Reserve Meritorious Service
63 Coast Guard Reserve Meritorious Service
64 Air Force Small Arms Expert Marksmanship

U.S.A.

SERVICE MEDALS

- 66 Civil War 1861–65
- 67 Indian Wars 1865–91
- 68 Spanish-American War 1898–99
- 69 Spanish War Service 1898–99
- 70 Cuban Occupation 1899–1902
- 71 Puerto-Rican Occupation 1899–1902
- 72 Philippine Congressional Medal
- 73 Philippine Campaign 1899–1913
- 74 China Relief 1900–01
- 75 Cuban Pacification 1906–09
- 76 Mexican Campaign 1911–17
- 77 1st Nicaraguan Campaign 1912
- 78 Dominican Campaign 1916
- 79 Haitian Campaign 1915, 1919–20
- 80 Mexican Border Service 1916–17
- 82 Victory Medal W.W.1
- 81 Victory Medal W.W.1
- 83, 84 Occupation of Germany 1918–23
- 85 2nd Nicaraguan Campaign 1926–33
- 86 Yangtze Service 1926–32
- 87 China Service 1937–39
- 88 American Defense Service
- 89 Navy Expeditionary Medal
- 90 Marine Corps Expeditionary Medal
- 91 American Campaign
- 65 Civil War Campaign Medal
- 92 European-African Middle Eastern Campaign
- 93 Asiatic-Pacific Campaign
- 94 Atlantic War Zone Bar – Merchant Marine
- 95 Mediterranean – Middle East War Zone Bar
- 96 Pacific War Zone Bar
- 97 Combat Bar Merchant Marine
- 98 Defense Bar Merchant Marine

PLATE 56

U.S.A.

SERVICE, GOOD CONDUCT, POLAR MEDALS, ETC.

99 Women's Army Corps Service Medal

101 Victory Medal W.W.2

102 Merchant Marine W.W.2 Victory Medal

103 Army of Occupation (Berlin airlift)

104 Medal for Humane Action

105 National Defense Service Medal

106 Korean Service

100 Victory Medal W.W.2

108 U.N. Service Medal Korea

109 U.N. Medal

110 Armed Forces Expeditionary Medal

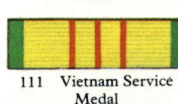
111 Vietnam Service Medal

112 Merchant Marine Vietnam Service Bar

113 Combat Readiness Medal

114 Navy Good Conduct Medal

115 Marine Corps Good Conduct Medal

116 Coast Guard Good Conduct Medal

117 Army Good Conduct Medal

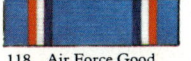
118 Air Force Good Conduct Medal

119 Civil Air Patrol Service Ribbon – 1500 hours

120 Dewey Medal Manila Bay 1898

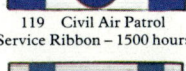
121 Sampson Medal West Indies 1898

122 Peary Polar Expedition Medal 1908–09

123 NC-4 Medal 1919

124 1st Byrd Antarctic Medal 1928–30

125 2nd Byrd Antarctic Medal 1933–35

126 U.S. Antarctic Service Medal 1939–41

127 Antarctica Service Medal

128 Bailey Medal

107 U.N. Service Medal Korea

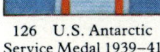

129 Philippine Defense

130 Philippine Liberation

131 Philippine Independence

132 American Typhus Commission

U.S.A.

LIFE SAVING MEDALS, MARKSMANSHIP MEDALS, ETC.

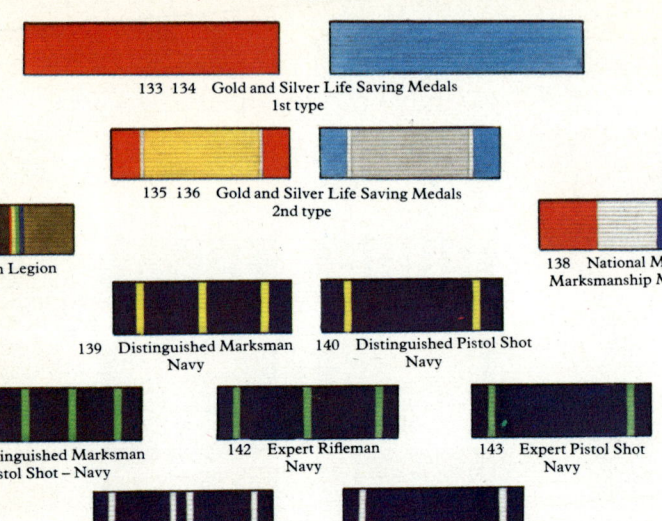

133 134 Gold and Silver Life Saving Medals
1st type

135 136 Gold and Silver Life Saving Medals
2nd type

137 American Legion

138 National Matches Marksmanship Medals

139 Distinguished Marksman Navy

140 Distinguished Pistol Shot Navy

141 Distinguished Marksman or Pistol Shot – Navy

142 Expert Rifleman Navy

143 Expert Pistol Shot Navy

144 Expert Rifleman U.S.C.G.

145 Expert Pistol Shot U.S.C.G.

AMERICAN RED CROSS SERVICE MEDALS

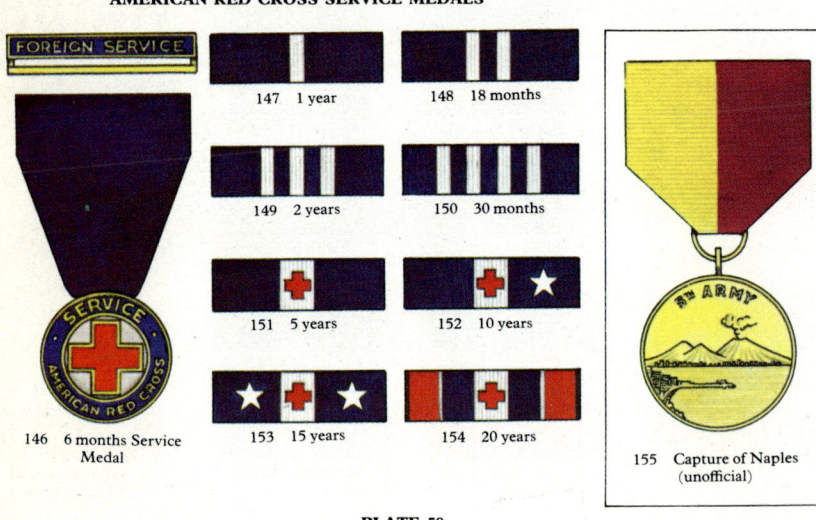

146 6 months Service Medal

147 1 year

148 18 months

149 2 years

150 30 months

151 5 years

152 10 years

153 15 years

154 20 years

155 Capture of Naples (unofficial)

PLATE 58

REPUBLIC OF VIETNAM

ORDERS, DECORATIONS AND MEDALS

2 Đệ-Nhất Đẳng
3 Đệ-Nhị Đẳng
4 Đệ-Tam Đẳng
5 Đệ-Tứ Đẳng
6 Đệ-Ngũ Đẳng
8 Lục-Quân Huân-Chương Đệ-Nhất Hạng
9 Lục-Quân Huân-Chương Đệ-Nhị Hạng
10 Không-Lực Huân-Chương Đệ-Nhất Hạng
11 Không-Lực Huân-Chương Đệ-Nhị Hạng
12 Hải-Quân Huân Chương Đệ I Hạng
13 Hải-Quân Huân-Chương Đệ II Hạng
14 Lục-Quân Vinh-Công Bội-Tinh
15 Không-Quân Vinh-Công Bội-Tinh
16 Hải-Quân Vinh-Công Bội-Tinh
1 Bảo-Quốc Huân-Chương 4. Đệ-Tam Đẳng
17 Biệt-Công Bội-Tinh
7 Quân-Công Bội-Tinh
18 Anh-Dũng Bội-Tinh với Nhành Dương Liễu
19 Anh-Dũng Bội Tinh với Ngôi Sao Vàng
20 Anh-Dũng Bội-Tinh với Ngôi Sao Bạc
22 Huy-hiệu Tuyên-Công Đơn-vị màu Ahn-Dũng Bội-Tinh với Ngôi Sao Vàng
21 Anh-Dũng Bội-Tinh với Ngôi Sao Đồng

PLATE 59

REPUBLIC OF VIETNAM

DECORATIONS AND MEDALS

23 với cánh Chim-Vàng

Phi-Dũng Bội-Tinh
24 với cánh Chim-Bạc

25 với cánh Chim-Đồng

26 với Neo-Vàng

Hải-Dũng Bội-Tinh
27 với Neo-Bạc

28 với Neo-Đồng

30 Nhân-Dũng Bội-Tinh

31 Trung-Chánh Bội-Tinh

Danh-Dự Bội-Tinh
33 Hạng I 34 Hạng II

Tham-Mưu Bội-Tinh
35 Hạng I 36 Hạng II

Kỹ-Thuật Bội-Tinh
37 Hạng I 38 Hạng II

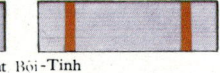
Huấn-Vụ Bội-Tinh
39 Hạng I 40 Hạng II

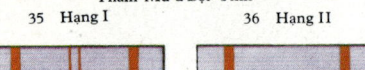

29 Ưu-Dũng Bội-Tinh

41 Chỉ-Đạo Bội-Tinh

42 Quân-Vụ Bội-Tinh

32 Chiến-Thương Bội-Tinh

45 Dân-Vụ Bội-Tinh Hạng I

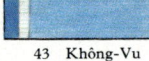
43 Không-Vụ Bội-Tinh

44 Hải-Vụ Bội-Tinh

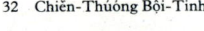
49 Nhất-Trí Bội-Tinh

46 Dân-Vụ Bội-Tinh Hạng II

47 Quân-Phong Bội-Tinh

48 Chiến-Dịch Bội-Tinh

50 Vị-Quốc Bội-Tinh

PLATE 60

KINGDOM OF YUGOSLAVIA

ORDERS, DECORATIONS AND MEDALS

2. Karadjordjeva Zvezda IV Reda
3. Karadjordjeva Zvezda sa mačevima
1. Karajordjeva Zvezda III Reda
4. Orden Beli Orao V Reda
5. Orden Svetog Save V Reda
6. Orden Jugoslovenska Kruna V Reda
7. Medalja za hrabrost
8. Medalja za vojničke vrline
9. Zlatna medalja za Revnosnu službu
10. Spomenica Srpsko-Turskog rata 1912
11. Spomenica Srpsko-Bulgarskog rata 1913
12. Medalja Kralja Petra I

PLATE 61

KINGDOM OF YUGOSLAVIA

MILITARY AND CIVIL MEDALS AND DECORATIONS OF SERBIA AND MONTENEGRO

13 Spomenica za oslobodjenje i ujedinjenje 1914–18
14 Albanska spomenica
15 Ratni krst spomenica 1941–45
16 Medalja za gradjanske zasluge
17 Orden Crvenog Krsta
18 Medalja Crvenog Krsta
19 Orden Takovskog Krsta III Reda
20 Orden Kneza Danila
21 Stara medalja za hrabrost
22 Obilića medalja

PLATE 62

SOCIALIST FEDERAL REPUBLIC OF YUGOSLAVIA

MILITARY ORDERS, DECORATIONS AND MEDALS

1. Orden narodnog heroja
2. Orden slobode
3. Orden ratne zastave
5. Orden partizanske zvezde drugog reda
4. Orden partizanske zvezde prvog reda
6. Orden partizanske zvezde trećeg reda
7. Orden narodne armije prvog reda
9. Orden narodne armije trećeg reda
8. Orden narodne armije drugog reda
10. Orden za vojne zasluge prvog reda
Orden za vojne zasluge
11. drugog reda
12. trećeg reda
13. Medalja za vojne zasluge
14. Orden za hrabrost
15. Medalja za hrabrost
16. Medalja za vojničke vrline

PLATE 63

SOCIALIST FEDERAL REPUBLIC OF YUGOSLAVIA

CIVILIAN ORDERS, DECORATIONS AND MEDALS

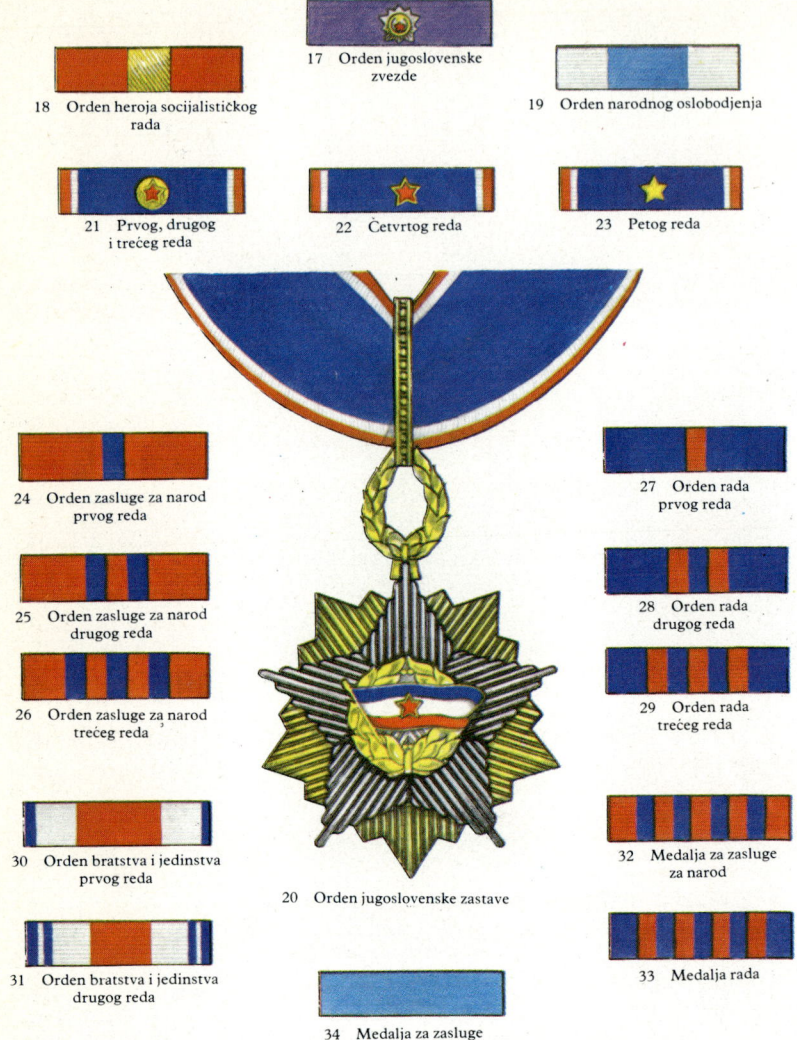

17 Orden jugoslovenske zvezde
18 Orden heroja socijalističkog rada
19 Orden narodnog oslobodjenja
21 Prvog, drugog i trećeg reda
22 Četvrtog reda
23 Petog reda
24 Orden zasluge za narod prvog reda
25 Orden zasluge za narod drugog reda
26 Orden zasluge za narod trećeg reda
27 Orden rada prvog reda
28 Orden rada drugog reda
29 Orden rada trećeg reda
30 Orden bratstva i jedinstva prvog reda
31 Orden bratstva i jedinstva drugog reda
20 Orden jugoslovenske zastave
32 Medalja za zasluge za narod
33 Medalja rada
34 Medalja za zasluge

PLATE 64

Belgium

Plate 1. Orders and Decorations

Belgium became an independent nation in 1830 and two years later the Order of Léopold (1) was instituted, named after the reigning King Léopold I.

The Order of the Crown (2), the Order of the African Star (14), the Order of the Lion (15) and the Order of Léopold II (13), instituted respectively in 1897, 1888, 1891 and 1900, were orders of Congo which was then an independent state. These orders became Belgian in 1908.

Basically each order is divided into five classes but there are considerable differences between them. For instance, in the case of the Order of the Crown the Grand Croix replaces the Grand Cordon which is the top class of the Order of Léopold only. The latter is divided into Titre Militaire, Titre Maritime and Titre Civil, the first two with crossed swords and crossed anchors, respectively, between the crown and the cross. The badges of the 5th Class (Chevalier) of all the orders are made of silver, all the others are of gold.

Medals of gold, silver and bronze are associated with the orders and a miniature of the medal is worn on their service ribbons, which is usually that of the corresponding order. However, the ribbon of the medals of the Order of the Crown has two additional white stripes. Gold and silver palms worn attached to the latter ribbon are also associated with the Order of the Crown and miniature replicas of these palms are worn on the service ribbons.

The Order of Léopold has no medals or palms but when awarded to civilians for special merit in war-time, a different ribbon, with one or two gold stripes, is used.

Palms with the royal monogram are a further distinction and can be worn on the ribbons of the Orders of Léopold and of the Crown.

Rosettes and gold-silver stripes of lace are attached to the centre of the service ribbons as a means of displaying the class of a particular order. The classes of the Belgian orders are as follows:

    (3) Grand Cross   rosette on gold stripe.
    (4) Grand Officer   rosette on silver-gold stripe.
    (5) Commander   rosette on silver stripe.
    (6) Officer   rosette.
    (7) Knight   plain ribbon.

The Military Cross (16) is awarded in two classes: the decoration of 1st Class rewards twenty-five years of distinguished commissioned officer's service while the 2nd Class is given for twenty-five years of service as a whole, including the period spent at the officers' school, etc. A rosette is worn on the ribbon of the Military Cross of 1st Class.

The Military Decoration for Acts of Heroism (18), also known as 'Article 4', is a bravery award for N.C.O.s and privates while the Décoration Militaire pour Ancienneté (19) is given to N.C.O.s after fifteen years of meritorious service and to privates after ten years.

Crosses and medals had already been awarded to civilians during World War I: the ribbon was sea green with 3 mm stripes of red, yellow and black, and black, yellow and red on either side. The ribbon of the crosses had an additional gold stripe (4 mm) in its centre. Later, two crosses, in gold and silver respectively, and gold, silver and bronze medals, were introduced as a reward for civil bravery during World War II (17).

Plate 2. War Medals

Although not all these ribbons refer directly to war campaigns, all are in one way or another connected with the events of war and therefore should be grouped together.

The first is the ribbon of the Franco-Prussian War, 1870–71 (20) the medal of which was issued in 1911, to eligible survivors. World War I broke out three years later and Belgium was invaded by the German Army; the subsequent struggle saw the introduction of a number of awards.

An oval, bronze medal with dark blue ribbon was given to War Volunteers (21) and in 1918 the Yser Medal (22) was awarded to the veterans of the 1914 Yser battle. Later, in 1934, the medal was replaced by a cross. In the same year the Croix du Feu (29) was distributed to all those who had served in the firing line during the war.

The Maritime Decoration (23) comprises gold and silver crosses, and gold, silver and bronze medals with a sea-green ribbon adorned with crossed anchors. The Medal of Queen Elisabeth (24) and of King Albert (25) were civilian awards, the former for women, established in 1916 and 1919 respectively.

The best-known award is the War Cross (27) which was instituted on 5 October 1915 to reward acts of bravery on the battlefield; mentions in despatches (citations) were shown on the suspension and on the service ribbons in the form of small Belgian Lions or palms (laurel branch) with King Albert's monogram, as listed below:

Bronze Palm	mention in Army despatch
Gilt Lion	mention in Divisional despatch
Silver Lion	mention in Brigade despatch
Bronze Lion	mention in Regimental despatch

A gilded palm replaced five silver palms, which in turn replaced five bronze palms.

The Commemorative Medal 1914–18 (28) was created on 21 July 1919 and the following devices could be worn on the ribbon:

Gilt crown	for volunteers
Silver bar	for front-line service
Gilt bar	replaces five silver bars
Red cross	for wounded
Silver star	for war disabled

The Political Prisoners (30) and those who during the war had suffered deportation (31) were rewarded by medals created some years after World War I. The Inter-allied Victory Medal (32) instead, was one of the first post-war creations, instituted on 14 July 1919, following a decision taken at the Peace Conference in the previous January, to create a truly international medal, with the same ribbon, to be awarded to all the war veterans of the nations of the Entente. This medal was given to all those mobilised between the dates of 1 August 1914 and 11 November 1918, including members of the Civil Guard on active duty and nurses of military hospitals.

The War Cross (33) was re-issued in 1941 to reward bravery during World War II. However, some details of the new cross were changed, the ribbon was different from that of the previous cross and although the citation badges remained the same the monogram '£' replaced 'A' on the palms.

The Commemorative Medal 1940–45 (34) could bear the following badges on its ribbon:

Crossed swords	for the 1940 campaign
Crossed anchors	for naval service
Red cross	for wounded
Bronze bar	for prisoners
Forks of lightning	for service of information
Gold star	for colonial public duties

A new medal was created for the War Volunteers 1940–45 (35) with a blue and red striped ribbon and a new Maritime Medal (36), still with crossed anchors on the ribbon, was instituted in 1941. A cross was awarded to Belgian ex-Political Prisoners (37) and a medal to the ex-Prisoners of War (38) as a token of recognition of their sufferings.

The patriots who refused to collaborate and work for the enemy were called Réfractaires and became eligible for a medal in 1951 (39). Green ribbons with yellow, white or red stripes are attached to this medal. World War II gave rise to the Resistance, which, although an ancient idea was developed along new lines. The Médaille de la Résistance (40) and the Médaille du Résistant Civil (41) were issued in consequence.

The Croix des Evadés (42) was instituted in 1944 by the Belgian

Government in the United Kingdom as a reward to those who had escaped from Belgium, from P.O.W. camps or political prisons. The escape, however, should have been considered to have had a patriotic merit.

The Abyssinian Campaign, 1941, (43) was commemorated by a medal and the two following ribbons (44, 45), with self-explanatory titles, recall the gallant colonial participation in the war effort. The Medal of Belgian Gratitude (46) is the last World War II award; in gold, silver and bronze versions it rewards merit for acts of mercy accomplished during the war.

The Médaille Commémorative des Théâtres d'Opérations Extérieurs (47) was awarded to Belgian personnel who took part in the Korean campaign, although officially this war is not mentioned in the medal's title.

The last two medals commemorate the Centenary of Belgian Independence and the memory of King Albert, the reigning monarch at the time of the Great War (48, 49).

Czechoslovak Socialist Republic

Plate 3. Order, Decorations and Medals

The Order of Clement Gottwald for the Construction of the Socialist Homeland (1) is the highest award for outstanding services to the nation and usually the recipient obtains, simultaneously, the Gold Star of Hero of the Czechoslovak Socialist Republic (2).

The star of the former order bears a small bust of President Gottwald in its centre and, as in the case of the Gold Star of Hero of the C.S.S.R. and the Gold Star of Hero of Socialist Labour (3), the actual decoration is worn in all circumstances; the service ribbon is never worn on its own.

The Silver Star of the Order of 25 February 1948 (4), the date on which Czechoslovakia became a socialist nation, is worn on its own without a ribbon, while lesser merits which could give access to this order are rewarded by silver and bronze medals (5) with deep red ribbon; the design of the medals reproduce the centrepiece of the silver star.

There is no metal decoration in the case of the two following awards: the Ribbon of Glory of the State Order of Clement Gottwald (6) and the Czechoslovak State Decoration of Vaclav Kopecky (7). A gilded laurel branch is attached to the ribbon of the former award.

Two enamelled badges, without ribbon, reward ten years of exemplary service in the People's Militia and are technically known as 1st Class and 2nd Class Decoration for Services, 10 Years in the People's Militia (8, 9). The actual badges are entirely different from each other.

The last four ribbons in this plate reward merits in the fields of industriousness and enterprise as follows: the highest award is the Order of the Red Banner of Labour (10), the metal decoration of which depicts a flying, red enamelled banner below a red star, both superimposed on the symbols of industry and agriculture, the cogwheel and wheatsheaf, and the lime leaves that are the traditional symbol of Czechoslovakia. A five-pointed red enamelled star suspended to the ribbon by a wreath of lime leaves is the decoration of the Order of the Red Star of Labour (11) while a silver medal with the same attachment is the Decoration for Labour Service (12) and a similar bronze medal, attached to its ribbon by a plain ring, is the Decoration for Labour Sacrifice (13). Their ribbons are 38 mm in width.

Plate 4. Decorations and Medals

Most of the modern Czechoslovak orders and decorations were instituted in the early 1950s, after a period of post-war resettlement, consequently both the Order of the Republic (14) and the Order of Labour (15) date back to 1951. The former, a coloured Czechoslovak banner flying above the hammer and sickle, and lime leaves on a background representing a bare brick wall, is awarded for distinguished services in many fields of national progress while the latter, which basically depicts a red star above a cogwheel and wheatear background, rewards specific merits in the cause of labour.

The two following ribbons stand for the Decoration for Merits in Advancement (16) and the Decoration for Outstanding Labour (17) which are both in the shape of medals, 33 mm diameter.

The Order of the Red Flag (18) and the Order of the Red Star (19) are military awards instituted in 1955; the Czech Lion, below a star, is the centrepiece of the reverse of the former and is also the obverse's centrepiece of the two following military medals: the Medal for Merit in the Defence of the Homeland (20) and the Medal for Service for the Homeland (21).

Jan Zizka of Trocnova was leader of the Hussites in the fifteenth century wars against the Germans and a national hero of independence. Therefore, a special order, dedicated to his name, was instituted in June 1946. There are three degrees of this military order: the Gold Star of the Czechoslovak Officers' Order of Jan Zizka of Trocnova (22); and the Silver Star and the Medal of the Czechoslovak Officers' Order of Jan Zizka of Trocnova (23). The stars of the first two degrees are badges with Zizka's head in the centre and eight spikes around while the medal shows only the hero's head surrounded by an inscription. Only the latter is attached to a ribbon, black with a central red stripe; the service ribbons of the stars are the same but with additional gold or silver crossed clubs, or batons attached to their centre. The same motif is present on the reverse of the medal, the service ribbon of which is plain.

Bravery on the battlefield and outstanding military services are rewarded by the Czechoslovak Military Order of the White Lion 'For Victory' (24) instituted in February 1945, as the highest military award. The order is basically divided in five grades: two stars, one cross and two medals, identified by miniature replicas of these on their corresponding service ribbons. The first two grades are silver eight-pointed stars, composed of rays bursting from the centre, an enamelled circle, with the Czechoslovak Lion surrounded by the inscription 'Za Víytézství' ('For Victory'). Two small gold or silver crossed swords appear at the feet of the lion to determine the class of the order, the Star of 1st Class or of 2nd Class, respectively.

The Cross of the order is made of red enamel with the same centrepiece as the stars, and the same motto on blue enamel. The gold and silver medals depict the centrepiece alone.

The Czechoslovak Cross of Valour of the 1914–18 War (25) was instituted in 1918, while the 1939 version of the same cross was instituted in 1940 to reward acts of bravery performed before and after the date of its institution, for the duration of World War II (26).

Three medals with different ribbons commemorate the Slovak Uprising of August 1944 (27, 28, 29): the medals of gold and silver are the 1st and 2nd Class of the order while the third, made of bronze, is known as the Commemorative Medal of the Slovak National Uprising.

Another award instituted in the 1940s, in 1948 precisely, is the Czechoslovak Decoration for Labour (30) which consists of three medals of 36 mm in diameter, in gold, silver and bronze all suspended from the same red ribbon. This is, of course, a civilian decoration and the recipient of a gold medal assumes the title of Hero of Labour.

The Decoration Medal of Jan Evangelist Purkyn (31) was instituted in 1954 to reward merits in the field of medicine and the medal has the Aesculapious Staff on the reverse. One year earlier, a decoration was created to reward merits in the field of pedagogy, psychology, and similar intellectual activities: this is the Decoration Medal of Jan Amos Komensky (32). The Decoration for Bravery (33) was instituted in 1951 and is a civilian award.

Plate 5. Decorations and Medals

The Czechoslovak Military Order 'For Liberty' was instituted in 1946 for Czechs and foreigners who participated in the War of Liberation. The Gold Star (34) is the first degree of this order, followed by a silver and bronze medal (35) which depict the centrepiece of the star, the soldiers' heads surrounded by the inscription 'For the Liberty of Czechoslovakia'. Miniature replicas of the decoration are worn on the service ribbon. The Czechoslovak Medal for Bravery Before the Enemy (36) is a 1940 award re-instated after World War II, in 1946, at the time when the Czechoslovak Janesik Medal (37) was instituted. The latter is an award for partisans. The Czechoslovak Military Medal for Merit in silver and in bronze (38) was created in 1943 by the Czech Government, then in exile. Silver or bronze crossed swords are worn on the service ribbons in order to distinguish the class of this award.

After World War II a number of medals were issued to commemorate battles in which Czech troops participated and national historical events: the Sokolov Commemorative Medal (39) was instituted in 1948 to commemorate the battle of March 1943 at Sokolov in Poland. The Zborov Commemorative Medal (40) was instituted in 1947: it is a silver medal with the bust of T. G. Masaryk on the obverse and the inscription 'Zborov 1917–1947' below flags and a laurel wreath on the reverse. The Bachmac Commemorative Medal was created in 1948 as an anniversary medal '1918–1948' (41). It should be noted that the colours of the Russian Saint George ribbon are present in the central part of the ribbons of the last two medals.

The Dukla Commemorative Medal (42) was created in 1959 to commemorate an action of 1944. The Czechoslovak Commemorative Military Medal (43) was instituted in London in 1943 for the conflict 1939–43. It consists of a wreath of lime leaves and a vertical sword in bronze, with the small silver Czech Lion at the bottom.

The Commemorative Badge of the Second National Uprising (44) is in reality a medal with a suspension ribbon, depicting the symbolical 'head' of the Republic and the inscription 'Za Vèrnost 1939–1945' (For Services 1939–1945) on the obverse and the medal's title on the reverse. The Czechoslovak Revolution Medal (45) was created in 1918 to commemorate the 1914–18 War by which Czechoslovakia achieved its independence.

The Commemorative Badge for Released Political Prisoners (46) is in reality a bronze cross which depicts the Czech Lion surrounded by a wreath of thorns on the obverse's centre, suspended to the ribbon by means of a plain ring. It was conferred on political victims of World War II. The Badge of the Czechoslovak Partisan (47) was instituted in 1946.

The Czechoslovak Order of the White Lion (48) was created in December 1922 as the highest national order of the new republic but the present order derives from the statutes of January 1961. It is divided in three classes, with a military and a civil division and is conferred on foreigners who have achieved special merit. The Collar of the order, usually reserved for heads of state, could be awarded in conjunction with the 1st Class of the order or on its own. The 1st Class Star of the order and a section of the sash have been illustrated; the badge depicts a silver

Czech Lion superimposed on a five-armed red enamelled cross encased in gold, with a lime leaf between each arm. This badge hangs from a gold lime leaves wreath which, in the case of the military division, bears crossed swords as well.

Kingdom of Denmark

Plate 6. Orders, Decorations and Medals

The Order of the Elephant (1) is one of the oldest orders of knighthood in Europe as it was founded *circa* 1457 and its badge, the Elephant, was adopted in 1580. Originally, only fifty knights could hold the appointment and all insignia, even today, must be returned after the death of the holder. The insignia consists of the badge of the order, attached to a collar, a star and another badge, attached to a sash ribbon 10 cm wide, worn across the left shoulder.

The Order of Dannebrog (2, 3) was instituted in 1671 and until 1808 it had only one class, reserved for fifty amongst the highest dignitaries and noblemen. In June 1808 the order was divided in four classes with an additional decoration, the Silver Cross, and could be conferred upon anyone eligible, regardless of rank and privilege. The statute and the insignia of the order was further modified later until finally, in 1952, the last class was divided in two grades, Knight of 1st Class and Knight, wearing a gold and a silver cross respectively, the former with a rosette on the ribbon.

Rosettes and gold and silver stripes of lace are worn on the service ribbons to identify the classes of the Order of Dannebrog, which at present are as follows:

Grand Commander

Grand Cross, which could also be awarded 'with diamonds'

Commander 1st Class and Commander; the former with a breast
    star as well as the cross on a neck ribbon

Knight 1st Class and Knight

The Medal of Merit (4) was instituted in 1845 and is still the highest Danish decoration. It can be awarded in gold or silver versions for good and loyal service to the nation. Its ribbon was initially 31 mm in width but was eventually reduced to 27 mm. Other medals were attached to the same ribbon, for instance the Medal for Heroic Deeds, a bravery award established in 1793, which was suspended by a 20 mm and later by a 31 mm ribbon. The same ribbon is attached to the Life Saving Medal (31 mm), the 'Ingenio et Arti' Medal (27 mm) and others.

A beautifully illustrated book on this subject is *Danish Orders and*

Medals by Captain P. J. Jørgensen; it is written in English and provides indispensable guidance for the enthusiast.

The first Danish war medal was struck on the occasion of the Battle of Copenhagen, in 1801, and although the gold medals had no suspension the silver version was attached to the above-mentioned ribbon, 20 mm wide. A new ribbon was made for the medals commemorating the wars to 1848–50 and of 1864 (5) against the Germans by which Prussia finally took over the Duchies of Holstein, Schleswig and Lauenborg.

King Christian X's Medal for participation in the War 1940–45 (6) was issued in 1946 and it is the final Danish war medal. The Korea Medal (15) was instituted in 1956 as a reward for personnel serving on the hospital ship Jutlandia which was engaged solely in its mission of mercy in Korean waters.

The Good Service Medals of the armed forces (7) all use the same ribbon. The Naval Good Service Medal was created in 1801 originally as a means of attracting men to work in the dockyards. In 1844 it was granted to petty officers and also to officers in 1925. The Good Service Medal for the Army was instituted in 1945, for the Air Force in 1953 and in the same year a medal was granted to the civilian employees of the Ministry of Défence. These medals are a reward for twenty-five years of good service.

The Police Good Service Medal (8) and the Civil Defence Good Service Medal (9) were adopted in 1959 and 1963 respectively. On the 4th of May, Good Service Medals are awarded yearly to members of the Home Guard (10) and a Distinguished Flying Medal (11) was instituted in 1962 to reward long service or gallantry of officers and airmen. A number of Good Service Medals are awarded to eligible firemen (12) according to the particular organisation, or fire brigade, they belong to; all the medals are suspended by the same yellow ribbon.

A light blue ribbon, 27 mm in width, identifies the Commemorative Badge of the Golden Wedding of King Christian IX and Queen Louise (13). Technically it is a household award, issued in 1892. The Schleswig Medal (14) commemorates the 1920 Plebiscite by which Schleswig returned to Denmark. The same ribbon was used for the Liberation Commemorative Medal instituted in 1946 by King Christian X.

The Honour Badge of the Danish Reserve Officers Organisation (16) was created in 1950 and the Honour Badge of the League of Civil Defence (17) in 1956.

Individuals who achieve special merit in the cause of tourism can be awarded the Danish National Travel Association Medal (18) and those who distinguish themselves at home or abroad for services in the field of handicrafts can become eligible for the Medal of Merit of the Chamber of Danish Handicraft (19)

The Danish Red Cross Badge of Honour and the Medal (20) were instituted in 1916 and 1927 respectively and were awarded until 1963 when the decorations were changed to include a beautiful pelican in the process of feeding her young. The Badge of Honour retained the previous ribbon while the new Service Medal and Service Medal 1st Class were given a new one (21) previously used for the commemorative medals for Aid to Prisoners of War 1914–19, for Aid to Sick and Wounded in the Finnish War 1939–40 and for Relief Work during World War II. The Danish Red Cross Commemorative Medal for Participation in the Exchange of Prisoners of War in Korea, 1953, (22) was awarded to nine doctors who took part in this mission.

Danish decorations and medals are usually suspended by crossed ribbons, similar to the Russian type of suspension, but some medals can also be attached to straight ribbons.

Republic of France

Plate 7. Orders and Decorations

The first French order was instituted in 1352 and subsequently many others were instituted to be bestowed upon the nobility of the time; they represented, therefore, a further privilege, rather more in fact than a reward for individual merit. The Royal Order of St Louis, founded in 1693 by King Louis XIV, was a military order which, eventually, was to reward military merit, regardless of class distinction.

The French Revolution abolished all privileges of birth and consequently the existing orders as well and in 1802 Napoleon Bonaparte, then a First Consul, instituted the Légion d'Honneur (1) as a reward for both civic virtue and military bravery. Originally the order was in four classes, with the following titles: Grand-Officier, Commandant, Officier and Chevalier. A fifth, top class, was added in 1805 originally under the title of Grand-Aigle, later to become known as Grand Cordon and finally, in 1814, as Grand Croix. In the same year the title of Commandeur replaced that of Commandant.

The insignia of the order was established by decree of 11 July 1805; it consisted of a white cross of five arms, superimposed on a laurel wreath and with the Emperor's effigy as its centre, in a round frame inscribed 'Napoléon Emp. des Français'. The French Eagle and the inscription 'Honneur et Patrie' was the centrepiece of the reverse.

In 1806 a crown was added at the top of the cross and several minor modifications were devised during the next few years. In 1814 the bust of King Henry IV, king of France and Navarre, replaced Napoleon's in the centre of the cross but the latter was reinstated in 1848, in the period of the Second Republic, which entailed the elimination of the crown. However, the crown was re-placed at the top of the cross in 1851 and finally it was superseded by the laurel and oak leaves in 1870, during the Third Republic.

Too many modifications and changes concern both the statute and the insignia of this order to be dealt with in this book. In fact they are so numerous that a book could be written on the Légion d'Honneur alone.

The Légion d'Honneur and all the other French orders are worn in the following manner:

The Grand Cross (2) is displayed by the wearing of a ribbon sash across the right shoulder to the left hip on which a gold enamelled cross of the Grand Cross is attached; it is similar to that of the Commander. A silver badge (Plaque) is worn on the left breast.

The Grand Officer (3) wears the badge on the right breast and the Cross of Officer on the left.

The Commander (4) wears the cross suspended on a neck ribbon, larger than the ribbons of the lower classes.

The Officer (5) wears the cross on the left breast as a medal, suspended on a straight ribbon (38 mm) on which a rosette is attached.

The Knight (6) wears a silver enamelled cross on the breast, attached on a plain straight ribbon. The frame-work of the cross of the higher classes is made of gold.

The badge is all made of silver and depicts the five-armed cross superimposed on a star, with the allegorical effigy of the French Republic in its centre. Obsolete versions exist with the French Eagle, Napoleon and Henry IV in the centre and different models of the fleur-de-lys, or different flags, in between the cross's arms, instead of the star.

The ribbons of the Légion d'Honneur are red. Rosettes and stripes of gold and silver lace are placed upon the service ribbons to identify the various classes of an order, as follows:

Grand Cross (Grand Croix) rosette above gold stripes
Grand Officer (Grand Officier) rosette above silver and gold stripes
Commander (Commandeur) rosette above silver stripes
Officer (Officier) rosette only
Knight (Chevalier) plain ribbon

The above rule applies to the service ribbons of all the French orders illustrated in the following plates and the same system has been adopted in many countries of the world.

The Ordre de la Libération was instituted by General de Gaulle in November 1940 and has one class only the members of which, the Compagnons de la Libération, wear the Cross of Liberation (7) i.e. the Cross of Lorraine mounted on a sword, the whole on a rectangular background shield. The black and green colours of the ribbon stand for mourning and hope respectively.

The Military Medal (8) was instituted by Louis-Napoleon Bonaparte in 1852 for rewarding exceptional deeds of valour performed by non-commissioned officers and rank and file, although senior generals and admirals are also eligible for this decoration in specific circumstances. The obverse of the original decoration showed the French Eagle clutching a round laurel wreath with Louis-Napoleon's head in its centre but later, in 1870, a trophy of arms replaced the eagle and the head of the French Republic replaced Napoleon's.

The War Cross 1914–18 (9) was established in April 1915 and crosses with different years inscribed on the reverse were awarded, the purpose of the cross being to reward individuals for specific acts of bravery. Citation badges were worn on the suspension and on the service ribbons of the same cross, as shown below:

Bronze Palm (laurel branch)   mention in Army despatch
Gilt Star   mention in Army Corps despatch
Silver Star   mention in Divisional despatch
Bronze Star   mention in Brigade, Regimental or similar unit's despatch

The silver palm was created by decree of 8 January 1917 in order to replace five bronze palms.

An identical decoration (11, 12) was instituted on 26 September 1939, with '1939' inscribed on the reverse and the first citations were recorded soon afterwards. However, a new War Cross (13) was established by the Vichy Government on 28 March 1941. The bronze cross is the same as the previous one but with the date '1939–1940' on the reverse and a green and black ribbon similar to that of the medal for the 1870–71 campaign. In 1943, General Giraud, then commander in chief, created a new War Cross with crossed flags on the obverse and the date '1943' on the reverse, suspended on the World War I pattern of ribbon. The War Cross 1939–1945 was also awarded after the war to towns and villages in recognition of their population's support of the Resistance, or as a token of national appreciation for exceptional hardship suffered during the war.

The War Cross (T.O.E. – des Théâtres d'Opérations Extérieurs) (10) came into being in 1921 as a reward for overseas service during and after World War I. Palms and stars were granted and worn on the ribbons, as described above.

The Combatant's Cross (14, 15) was established by law of 1930 and was given to all those in possession of the combatant's card: the Vichy Government instituted the Combatant's Cross 1939–1940 (16) in 1941, but the latter was abolished in 1944 and in 1948 the use of the 1930's cross was also extended to World War II combatants.

The Cross of Volunteer Combatants (17) of World War I was instituted in 1935 while the Cross for Voluntary Military Service (21, 22) is one year older, and was given to officers and N.C.O.s of the reserve on duty during periods of voluntary training. Gold, silver and bronze crosses were awarded; the gold cross had a rosette on the ribbon. Wings identified service with the Air Force and an anchor, on the ribbon, identified naval service.

In 1926 a medal was created for escaped prisoners of war (18); later given to civilians as well. The same medal was conferred during World War II

The Resistance Medal (19) and the Medal for Volunteers of the Resistance (20), later to become a cross, have similar ribbons. The former was adopted in 1943, the latter after the war.

The Medal of French Gratitude (23) was instituted in 1917 as an acknowledgement to those who willingly, on their own initiative, brought aid to other people or acted in the public interest. It was awarded in three classes, gold with a rosette on the ribbon, silver with a blue enamel star on the ribbon, and bronze.

The Order of Merit of Black Africa (24) was instituted by the Vichy Government.

Plate 8. Orders of Merit

The Légion d'Honneur soon was proved inadequate to reward all the civil and military merits but Napoleon's reign was too brief to produce any alternative. The Academic Palms (34), earlier known as Palmes Universitaires, were devised in 1808 as badges of honour and not as what we regard today as a decoration. These badges were embroidered in gold, silver or white and blue silk and were worn on the left side of the coat. The rules governing this honour were changed eventually and finally, in 1866, gold and silver metal palms, suspended on a ribbon, were adopted. Subsequently, more modifications occurred in the 1920s and the Order of the Academic Palms, with its three classes was created in 1955.

The Order for Agricultural Merit (26) was established in 1883: initially there were only Knights of the Order but in 1887 the class of Officer was granted and in 1900 Commander as well.

Although many medals were created in the meantime for rewarding civil merits it was not until 1930 that the Order of Maritime Merit (30, 31) was instituted and others soon followed. The Order of Social Merit (32, 33) replaced the medals of Mutualité, Prévoyance Sociale and Assurances Sociales in 1936. The Order of Public Health (28) in 1938 replaced previous medals awarded for services to public assistance and hygiene and to the protection of infants. The Order of Commercial Merit (27) was instituted in May 1939.

After World War II a number of new orders were established, commencing with the Order of Merit for Artisans (29) in 1948, the Order of Touristic Merit (35) the year after. All the remaining orders came into being during the 1950s and are as follows:

Order of Combatant Merit (36)	14 September 1953
Order of Postal Merit (37)	14 November 1953
Order of the National Economy (38)	6 January 1954
Order of Merit of Sport (39)	6 July 1956
Order of Merit of Work (40)	21 January 1957
Order of Military Merit (41)	22 March 1957
Order of Civil Merit (42)	2 May 1957
Order of 'Arts and Lettres' (43)	2 May 1957
Order of Saharian Merit (44)	4 March 1958

Each of these orders is divided into three classes, Commanders, Officers and Knights who wear the decorations on a neck ribbon, on the breast with a rosette on the ribbon and without rosette respectively. Rosettes and gold/silver stripes of lace are applied to the service ribbons which, like the average French ribbons are 37–38 mm in width.

By the end of the 1950s the situation had moved to the opposite extreme; there were too many orders of merit and therefore in 1963 General de Gaulle instituted the National Order of Merit (45, 25), divided into five classes, which replaced the vast majority of the previous, minor orders. The National Order of Merit ranks after the Military Medal which in turn is third, after the Order of Liberation, and the Légion d'Honneur.

Plate 9. War Medals

As the wearing of service ribbons is a relatively modern custom there is no such ribbon in existence for a number of French medals; for instance the case of the Cross and Medal of July 1830, awarded to citizens who had distinguished themselves during 27, 28 and 29 July 1830. The original crosses and medals were attached to a light blue ribbon with two red side stripes, later changed to three equal stripes of red, blue and red. The Medal of St Helena was given to surviving veterans of the Napoleonic armies in 1858, attached to a 32 mm ribbon similar to that of the 1914–18 War Cross. A silver medal was given to those who were wounded on 22, 23 and 24 February 1848; it has a red ribbon edged on the right side by narrow stripes of white and blue.

The Crimea Medal (46) and the Baltic Medal (47) were British awards given to Frenchmen during the war against Russia and were recognised and accepted by the French government in 1856 and 1857 respectively.

The Médaille du Dragon or du Mérite (48) was instituted by the Emperor of China in 1863 and awarded in gold or silver versions to French servicemen who took part in the quelling of the Taï-Pings and, in the same year the medal of Mexico (49) was awarded to French troops aiding Emperor Maximilian of Mexico. He awarded the Mexican Military

Medal, the ribbon of which was red with two white side stripes. The 1859 campaign in Italy was commemorated by a medal (50) which was also given to Italians while Sardinian medals were earned by Frenchmen during the same war against Austria.

In 1868 official permission was granted for wearing a cross which was awarded by Pope Pius IX to all members of the French Expeditionary Corps who had taken part in the battle of Mentana where Garibaldi was defeated on 3 November 1867 (51). On 9 November 1911 a bronze commemorative medal was approved for surviving veterans who had been under arms in France or Algeria between July 1870 and February 1871 inclusive (52).

The following medals, made all of silver, commemorate French colonial campaigns which took place before the outbreak of World War I. The Tonkin Medal 1883–85 (53) was created in 1885 and later rewarded service in Indochina until 1895; the China Medal 1900–01 was suspended on the same yellow and green ribbon of the former.

An unusual ribbon, horizontally divided into green and light blue stripes, identifies the Madagascar campaign of 1885–86 and the subsequent 1895 expedition on the island (54). The Tonkin Medal, Madagascar 1885–86, Dahomey 1892 (55) and the Sudan Medal (56) all have the same obverse, while the Madagascar Medal 1895 is altogether different. The Maroc Medal (59) was awarded to all those who participated in the military operations that took place there between 1807 and 1809. Later, the same medal was awarded for service in Maroc until 1912, but in this case the bar 'Maroc' was worn on its ribbon. Later service was rewarded by the Colonial Medal (57). This medal was instituted in 1893 for participation in military operations in the colonies and protectorates. Clasps are usually present on its ribbon although medals with no clasps were awarded for long service. The following are clasps made of gold:

De l'Atlantique à la Mer Rouge – Mission Saharienne – Congo Gabon – Centre Africain

The following were made in silver:

Adrar – Afrique – Afrique Equatoriale Française – Afrique Française Libre – Afrique Occidentale Française – Algérie – Asie – Bir-Hacheim 1942 – Cochinchine – Comores – Congo – Côte d'Ivoire – Côte d'Or Côte des Somalis 1940–1941 – Dahomey – Erythrée – Ethiopie – Extrême-Orient Fezzan – Fezzan Tripolitaine – Guinée Française – Guyane – Haut-Mékong-Haut-Obanghi – Iles Marquises – Iles de la Societé – Laos et Mékong – Lybie – Madagascar – Maroc – Maroc 1925 – Maroc 1926 – Mauritanie – Nossi-Bé Nouvelle Caledonie – Sahara – Sénégal et Soudan – Somalie – Sud Tunisien – Sud Oranais – Tchad – Tonkin – Tunisie – Tunisie 1942–1943.

Tiny clasps are worn on the service ribbons as well, as illustrated. The Commemorative Medal of the 1914–18 war (59) was created in 1920, while the ribbons for wounded (60, 61) were instituted during the war: that for soldiers in July 1917 and the ribbon for civilians in July 1918. Red stars for each wound are worn on the former, silver stars on the latter.

The Inter-allied Victory Medal (62) with its usual rainbow-coloured ribbon was instituted in 1922. The idea of creating an international medal was first mooted by M Bouilloux-Lafont at the Chamber of Deputies and later Marshal Foch suggested its creation to the members of the Peace Conference. His proposition was accepted on 24 January 1919.

In June 1921 a bronze medal was instituted to reward the sacrifices of political prisoners and war hostages, classified as 'victims of the German invasion' (63); the Medal for French Fidelity (64) was created the following year for civilians of Alsace Lorraine who suffered imprisonment or exile because of their attachment to France. A star was worn on the ribbon for each year of imprisonment or exile.

In 1936 a new medal (65) was instituted for civilians of all German occupied provinces who had been imprisoned or deported.

The Commemorative Medal of Upper Silesia (66) was instituted by the Inter-allied Commissions of the Government and Plebiscite of that region and was officially sanctioned by the French Government in July 1922. In the same year the Levant Medal (67) was created for those who participated in the military operations in Syria-Cilicia between November 1918 and October 1921. Later issues of the medal had the clasp 'Levant 1925–1926'.

Since 1917 motions were raised in Parliament for the approval of a medal commemorating the Dardanelles Expedition but a decision was not reached until 1926 when one medal only was created with two different ribbons to identify the Orient Medal (68) and the Dardanelles Medal (69) respectively.

The next, a beautiful bronze medal, was instituted by the Government of Lebanon and French servicemen received it for helping to quell the post-war rebellion (70). It was approved by the French Government in June 1927.

Thus we arrive at World War II, for which a commemorative medal (71) was instituted in 1946, with the following clasps:
France – Norvège – Afrique – Italie – Libération – Allemagne – Extrême-Orient – Grand-Bretagne – U.R.S.S. – Atlantique – Méditerranée – Manche – Mer du Nord.

It should be noted that variations of the same clasp have been illustrated on the service ribbons of the Colonial Medal and of the World War II Medal in order to emphasise that different types of these clasps could be found. The full title of the following medal is Médaille Commémorative des Services Volontaires dans la France Libre (72) and was instituted in 1946 as well. A silver Cross of Lorraine was worn on the ribbons.

The Commemorative Medal of the Italian Campaign 1943–1944 (73) was approved in 1953 and its ribbon follows the pattern of that of the 1859 Medal. The Medal of Free France (74) is intended as a victory medal and thus is attached to a ribbon similar to that of the World War I Victory Medal but with inverted colours. The Medal of Conscripted Patriots (75) was adopted in 1954 to reward civilians of specific regions who, because of their attachment to France, had been subjected to deportation to any enemy country, i.e. Germany.

Plate 10. War Medals
All French citizens who had been deported or interned by the enemy during World War II became eligible for a medal in 1948 and the year after two ribbons were adopted, one for each qualification (76, 77). By a law of August 1948 the term 'deportation' refers in this case to citizens who because of acts of resistance had been taken to an enemy country for imprisonment while internment technically means imprisonment inside French territory. Another medal also with two ribbons (78, 79) was adopted in 1948 for the benefit of citizens who had been deported or interned for political reasons only, i.e. they were not necessarily resisting or opposing enemy occupation.

The Indochina Medal (80) was instituted in 1953 with a ribbon similar to that of the old Tonkin Medal, but with colours inverted. The French Commemorative Medal of the U.N.O. Operations in Korea (81) was instituted in 1952 to reward the honourable service performed by the French Battalion during that war.

Medals of Honour
The medals were created to reward distinguished achievements and merit or irreproachable long service, beyond the scope of the major awards. Many of these medals were in existence long before the orders of merit, which eventually replaced some of them.

The Honour Medal of Military Medical Service was instituted in 1931 in four classes, gold, gilt, silver and bronze. Later, in 1947 a special medal was created for personnel of the Navy (82) with a blue anchor woven in the centre of the ribbon and, in 1948, a medal was adopted for eligible personnel of the Air Force (83) as well; the latter with wings woven on the ribbon. It appears that the ribbon initially used had a wider red stripe in the centre.

The gold, silver and bronze Honour Medals of the Social Insurances (84, 85) were adopted in 1923 to reward special efforts in the field of social security; a rosette was worn on the ribbon of the gold medal. In 1936 the Order of Social Merit, in turn now obsolete, replaced these awards. Also there were two ribbons for the now obsolete Honour

Medals of Physical Education and Sport (86, 87) and a rosette was attached to the ribbon of the gold medal.

The Honour Medal of Waterways and Forests (88) was instituted in 1883 by the Ministry of Agriculture while the medals of the Customs (89) and Contributions Indirectes (90) were created in 1883 and 1894, respectively, by the Ministry of Finances.

The Honour Medal of Municipal and Rural Police (91) was created in 1903 and in 1936 it was re-titled Honour Medal of the French Police. A silver star is added on the ribbon if the medal was awarded for bravery. It should not be confused with the Médaille de la Gendarmerie Nationale (92) which was instituted in 1949 and is awarded for special merits, each citation identified by a grenade on the ribbon.

The skill of teaching has been rewarded since 1818 and the statute of these awards was modified innumerable times. The origins of the Medal for First Degree of Teaching (93) also known as Médaille des Instituteurs, can be traced to a law of 1886 which granted an Honourable Mention, a silver medal or a bronze medal to eligible teachers. The ribbon is worn with the silver medal. The Médaille de L'Education Surveillée (94) was created in April 1945 by the Ministry of Justice as a long service award for prison personnel.

The administration of the mines of the Sarre created awards for its own personnel in 1921. There were gilt, silver and bronze medals suspended on a light blue ribbon with yellow edges. The Medal of the Mines (95) was instituted by the Ministry of Industry and Commerce in 1953 and it is awarded in gold for thirty years of service, in silver-gilt for twenty years and in silver for fifteen years. A rosette is worn on the ribbon of the silver-gilt medal and a rosette on a small black and orange bar on that of the gold medal.

The Médaille d'Honneur de la Voir Départementale et Communale (Departmental and Communal Roads) was instituted in 1898 and the ribbon of this silver medal was identical to those illustrated in the next plate for the railways and aeronautics. The Médaille d'Honneur Departementale et Communale (96) was born in 1945 to reward long service of local administration employees and replaces the previous, the Médaille d'Honneur des Octrois (Plate 11, 106), des Halles et Marchés (same ribbon as 108, 109) and the Médaille d'Honneur des Employés Communaux (103). The medal is in gold, silver-gilt and silver and a rosette on silver lace is worn on the ribbon of the first (forty-five years' service), a rosette on that of the silver-gilt medal (thirty-five years) while the ribbon of the silver one is plain (twenty-five years).

The next, blue, white and red ribbon (97) was used for the Médaille d'Honneur des Affaires Etrangères, an award instituted during the Third Republic and for the Médaille des Epidémies which, in four classes, was created in 1885 just after a lethal epidemic had swept through France.

The Medal of Honour of the Musical and Choral Societies (98) was instituted in 1924 and that of the Postal and Telegraph's Service (99) in 1882. The ribbon of the latter was originally composed of seven tricoloured bands but since 1902 only six bands appear in this ribbon. The medal is awarded in gold, silver and bronze, the first two with a rosette on the ribbon.

Plate 11. Medals of Honour
The Médaille d'Honneur Pénitentiaire (100) was established in 1896 as a long service award for prison personnel and the colonial version of this award (101) was introduced two years later. The Médaille des Prud'hommes (102), now obsolete, was instituted in 1828, and originally was worn attached to a black neck ribbon. The Honour Medal of Communal (Council) Employees (103) was created in 1921 to reward thirty years of service; it is now obsolete.

The Medal of Public Assistance (104) instituted in 1891 and the Medal of Public Hygiene (105) created in 1923, were both replaced by the Order of Public Health in 1938. Both were in three classes, gold, silver and bronze, with a rosette worn on the ribbon of the first.

The Médaille d'Honneur des Octrois (106) established in 1904 is another award now obsolete. The Medal of the French Family (107), created in 1920 is in three classes, in gold for mothers who 'worthily' raised ten children, in silver for eight and bronze for five children. A bow of ribbon can be worn instead of the bronze medal, a rosette instead of the silver medal and a rosette on a bow instead of the gold medal.

Tri-coloured ribbons of seven vertical stripes are used for the Honour Medal of Public Works, of Aeronautics (109), of the Metropolitan and Overseas Railways (108). The first named was instituted in 1897, the Railways Medal in 1913 and the Aeronautics Medal in 1921. Devices are worn on the ribbons in order to identify the awards.

The Médaille de l'Aéronautique (110) was instituted in February 1945 to reward the professional skill or bravery of civil and military personnel; its ribbon is royal blue. The Honour Medal of Firemen (111), instituted in 1900, could be awarded for long service or for acts of bravery.

The following six ribbons have not existed since 1936, when the Order of Social Merit replaced these awards. The Médaille de la Prévoyance Sociale (112–114) was created in 1922 and the Médaille d'Honneur de la Mutualité (115–117) has existed since 1852 in gold, silver and bronze versions.

Most of the ribbons already dealt with were not worn as service ribbons and have been reported for the purpose of historical interest only. The same applies to the last four ribbons illustrated. The Honour Medal of Work (121) instituted in 1886 was an award for workers of industry and commerce, but in 1894 a special version of the same award was created for civilian workers of the Navy (118). In 1906 a black anchor was added on to the tri-coloured ribbon. A smaller blue anchor is present on the ribbon of the Honour Medal of the Mercantile Marine (119) and a red anchor is woven into the centre of the ribbon of the Maritime Life Saving Honour Medal (120). However in the case of the latter, the anchor is embroidered in gold on the ribbon of the gold medal. The Honour Medal of Agriculture (121) was instituted in 1883, and the Médaille d'Honneur de la France d'Outre-Mer in January 1932.

Plate 12. Colonial Orders and Decorations (Africa)

Most of the following orders and decorations are now obsolete and the few which still exist at present are known as Ordres de la France d'Outre-Mer. They rank as the French orders, usually in five classes, with rosettes and stripes on gold/silver lace on the service ribbons, as shown in the case of the Etoile Noire du Bénin (122–127). This order was created by King Toffa of Dahomey in 1889 and became a French colonial order in 1896.

The Nichan El Anouar (128) of which the star of officer has been illustrated, was instituted by Hamed ben Mohamed, Sultan of Tadjourah, in 1887: as the previous, it became a French colonial order in 1896. The Ordre de l'Etoile de Comore (130) is now obsolete while the Etoile d'Anjouan (129), another order of the Comores, is still in existence: it was founded in 1874 and reorganised by Sultan Mohamed Saïd Omar in 1892.

The Nichan Iftikhar (131) and the Ahed El Aman (132) also known as Nichan El Ahed, were Tunisian Orders created in the 1830s and 1860 respectively. The former, originally was only given by Mustapha Bey to high ranking ministers but by the beginning of the present century it was usually bestowed as a long service award. It was divided into five classes with an additional minor rank of Knight of 2nd Class, reserved for soldiers, spahis and minor officials. The Long Service Medal of the Tunisian Police (140) was instituted in 1927.

The Ouissam Alaouite (134, 135) was a Moroccan order created in 1913 to replace the order of Ouissam Hafidien (133) instituted only three years earlier. Amongst the Moroccan decorations I would like to mention the medals of Military and Civil Mérite Chérifien (138, 139), created in 1910 and 1924 respectively. The ribbons of some others have been illustrated in the next plate.

Plate 13. Colonial Orders and Decorations (Africa and Asia)

The Moroccan medal of the Police Chérifienne (142) was a long service award adopted in 1924. The Peace of Morocco Medal (144) was a Spanish medal recognised by the French Government in 1930, given to French and native soldiers who took part in the operation in North Morocco between 1 July 1925 and 25 July 1927.

The Médaille du Mérite Libannais (141) was created by the Government of Lebanon in 1922 and consists of four classes, with and without palms. The Honour Medal of Syrian Merit (146) was instituted in 1926 by the French High Commissioner in Syria. As the previous it is divided into four classes: gold with gold palms, silver-gilt with silver palms and silver and bronze medals without palms.

The Médaille du Mérite Indigène (or Mérite Malgache) (147) was instituted in 1901 by the C. in C. and Governor of Madagascar. Gold, silver and bronze medals were awarded, the first two with a rosette on the ribbon. The Madagascar Honour Medal for Work (148) was adopted in 1920, in silver and bronze versions only.

The following orders and decorations belonged to French Indochina and many have been subsequently adopted by the modern Indochinese nations.

The Order of the Dragon of Annam (Ordre du Dragon Vert) was founded at Hué by the Emperor Dong-Khang on 14 March 1886 as a reward for military and civil merit. It was divided into five classes and while the Europeans wore their decorations with green and yellow ribbon (149) the Annamites wore them with red and yellow ribbon (150).

The Military Medal (151) conferred on natives for bravery on the battlefield was different from its French version and some Indochinese characters were embroidered on the ribbon. One among many medals awarded by the Governor General was the Médaille de la Garde Indigène (157) which was instituted in 1929. The Medal of Customs and Excise (152) was adopted in 1900, that of the Forestry Service (159) in 1928 and the Medal of Medical Assistance in 1931 (158). Other medals existed but usually they were attached to the ribbon worn by their French counterparts.

The Annamite decorations were traditionally classified as Khan, Boï, Tien and Baï. The Ngoc-Khan was the highest decoration, made of jade, while the Kim-Khan (153) was made of gold and divided in four classes. The Boï (154) and Tien (155) were also divided into classes (Kim means gold) while the Baï, created by Emperor Gia Long in 1802 was a very rare decoration infrequently awarded. These were not the usual European type of decoration but were plaques of precious metal, beautifully engraved, worn on the chest suspended by means of a red cord around the neck.

Plate 14. Colonial Orders and Decorations (Asia)

The Royal Order was instituted by Norodom I, King of Cambodia, in

1864 and consists of five classes, the insignia and ribbons of which are worn in the usual French manner. Cambodians wear the ancient red and green ribbons (161) while Europeans wear white and yellow ribbons (160). The Order of Muniséraphon (162), founded in 1905, was a literary, historical and scientific award and the ribbon could only be worn attached to the badge, known as palms of merit.

The Order of Sowathara (163), in three classes, was founded in 1923 as an award in the field of agriculture. In order to become a commander of this order, the eligible individual had to be an officer, and previously a knight. There were gold and silver medals of Sisowath I (164) and later the Monivong Medals (165), named after the new king, replaced the former. All the other ribbons illustrated in this plate, down to No. 178 were Cambodian.

The Ordre du Million d'Eléphants et du Parasol Blanc (179) was instituted by Sisavang Vong, King of Luang-Prabang (Laos) in 1909. Three white elephants' heads under a parasol is the centrepiece of the insignia of the order of which, until 1927, there was only one class, later expanded to four. The Kingdom Medal (180), in three classes, depicts the effigy of King Sisavang Vong while the medals of Civic Merit (181) and Agricultural Merit (182), both extremely beautiful, depict Laotian personnages in their centre. The ribbons of the medals of Public Education (183) and of the Resistance (184) belonged to Laos as well.

The last two were ribbons of the Thai Federation; that for Civil Merit (185) was attached to a diamond-shaped decoration formed by four crosses of coloured enamel, joining into a central square. A sixteen pointed star was suspended on the other ribbon, of Military Merit (186).

German Empire

Plate 15. Orders, Decorations and Medals

The extent of this book prevents me from including the ribbons of the German States which, however, have been dealt with by Donald G. Neville in his recent brilliant publication *Medals, Ribbons and Orders of Imperial Germany and Austria*. Following the re-structuring of Germany, it is apparent that the ribbons of the German States were not only worn during the period of the Empire but that ribbons of the period were even worn during World War II. By 1945 all these ribbons were rendered obsolete and new ones were created eventually.

German suspension ribbons were 25, 30 and 35 mm in width; sash and neck ribbons were, of course, larger still. Service ribbons were mounted on a convex metal bar, with holes in its centre to affix eventual badges. These bars were usually 17 mm in length although 9·5 mm bars could be used as well.

Originally two lengths of ribbon were twisted around the mounting bar for each decoration (7) thus creating a beautiful effect, but later the fashion of straight 15 mm ribbons prevailed. The ribbon bar illustrated (7) obviously belonged to a Bavarian officer because his second ribbon is that of the Bavarian Military Order of Merit (1866), the fourth stands for an award of the Prince Regent, Léopold, and the last is a Bavarian long service ribbon. In many cases just a glance at a ribbons' bar would ascertain the nationality of its wearer because of the predominant colours of his ribbons. Light blue and white were the predominant colours of Bavarian ribbons, a great deal of dark crimson distinguished a ribbons' bar of the House of Saxe and light crimson prevails in the ribbons of Hesse. Mecklenburg's ribbons were usually light blue, crimson and yellow while dark blue and red were present in all the ribbons of Oldenburg. However, due to the complexity of this subject no hasty identification is advisable, nor could it be attempted without the help of a reliable reference book.

Prussia was the co-ordinator of German unification, thus its decorations became part of the national heritage while the other States' awards gradually fell into disuse.

The 'Order Pour le Mérite' (1) traces its origins to the Order of Generosity instituted in the 1660s, renamed in 1740. This Prussian order became the highest bravery distinction of the German Empire and could be awarded with, or without gold oak leaves. The cross was always worn around the neck.

Two ribbons of the Cross of Honour of the World War 1914–18 have been illustrated: the former was that of the combatants (2) while the latter, with its colours inverted, was for the widows and relatives of the fallen (3). The Iron Cross is the best-known German decoration. It was instituted in Prussia in 1831 by Frederick William III and remained a Prussian award until 1939. It was founded to reward military and civilian bravery during the war against Napoleon and was re-issued for the 1870–71 Franco-German War and for the third time during World War I, and the latter cross, 1st Class, has been illustrated (4). It was awarded as an order, in two classes and an additional Grand Cross. The Iron Cross, 1st Class, was worn pinned on the breast while the 2nd Class was suspended on a ribbon. A black ribbon with two white side stripes was used by Combatants (5) and a white ribbon with black stripes by Non-combatants (6). A miniature replica of the Iron Cross was worn on the ribbon to signify that the recipient was awarded the same decoration in the 1870–71 and 1914–18 wars (8).

The Emperor William Centenary Medal (9) was awarded in 1897 and the China Medal (10) in 1901, following the international expedition 1900–01 in China. The South-West Africa Medal (11) and Colonial Medal (12) were instituted in 1907 and 1912 respectively. The suspension ribbon of the latter medal for natives was only 30 mm, instead of 35 mm wide.

The following ribbon commemorates one of the post-World War I campaigns, in this case against Poland, for the possession of Silesia and this award, in two classes, was also known as the Silesian Eagle (13), instituted in 1919.

The Hanseatic Cities of Bremen, Lubeck and Hamburg each issued a cross for World War I service (14–16) while the Baltic Cross (17) was instituted in 1919 during the campaign fought at the time of the birth of the Baltic States.

German Third Reich

Plate 16. Orders and Decorations
The Third Reich came into existence with the advent to power of the National Socialist party and terminated at the end of World War II. During this period everything was centralised in accordance with the idea of a state within a party, new awards were devised and some existing ones modified.

The Meritorious Order of the German Eagle (18–20) was instituted in 1937 as a German national order capable of rewarding eminent foreign personalities. Initially it was divided into six grades, the Grand Cross of the order, the order with Star, a 1st, 2nd and 3rd Class and a silver Medal of Merit. In 1937 Italy's Mussolini was awarded the Grand Cross of the order With Diamonds, a unique grade, and in 1939 the Grand Cross in Gold was instituted and since then any class of the order could be awarded without (19) or with, swords (20). The order was modified in 1943 to make up a Grand Cross in Gold, a Grand Cross, five classes and silver and bronze medals. The service ribbon of the silver medal with swords, with a white stripe in its centre, has been illustrated (20). The sash ribbon of the original Grand Cross (1937–43) was 100 mm in width but several other suspension ribbons existed as well (See bibliography: *Orders, Decorations, Medals and Badges of the Third Reich.*)

The Iron Cross (21–23) was reinstated in September 1939, with new awarding grades, a modified appearance and a new ribbon. Further modifications to its statute led finally to the following grades: the Grand Cross of the Iron Cross, the Knight's Cross with Gold or Silver Oak Leaves, Swords and Diamonds, with Oak Leaves with, and without

Swords, the Knight's Cross, and the Iron Cross of 1st and 2nd Class. The latter has been illustrated twice, suspended from a German ribbon (22) and on Plate 18, suspended from a triangular Austrian ribbon (64). To follow the usual custom, each higher award could be given only to recipients of the lower grade.

A 'bar' in the form of the eagle and swastika above the date '1939', was given to recipients of a World War II Iron Cross already in possession of the 1914–18 version. The bar was worn above the breast cross of 1st Class or, in reduced size on the black and white ribbon of the Iron Cross 2nd Class.

The ribbon of the latter, of both wars, could also be worn from the 2nd buttonhole of the tunic. Personnel of the Army, Navy and Air Force whose acts of bravery were registered in the official Roll of Honour, wore distinctive badges (Clasps of Honour) on the above ribbon during the last two years of the war.

The War Merit Cross (25–27) was instituted in October 1939 as a reward for military merit, contrary to the Iron Cross which was purely an award for bravery. There were gold and silver variations of the Knight's War Merit Cross, worn suspended on a 45 mm neck ribbon, the Cross of 1st Class which was worn on the breast and the 2nd Class award which was attached to a ribbon and worn as a medal; all these grades could be awarded with or without swords. The lowest grade was represented by a bronze medal which depicted the cross in relief: its ribbon had a red stripe in the centre (27).

The German Order (24) was the highest award for German nationals; it was probably first bestowed in 1942 but it seems never to have developed, probably due to the pressures of war. The centrepiece of the cross depicts the N.S.D.A.P. badge and the cross was always worn on a neck ribbon or without ribbon, on the breast.

The German Red Cross (28) instituted its own decorations in 1922 which were modified in 1934, 1937 and in 1939. The final statute also renamed these awards Social Welfare decorations.

A decoration in two classes and a medal were instituted in 1936 in commemoration of the Olympic Games held in Berlin. The 1st Class decoration was distinguished by a metal eagle on the service ribbon (29).

Plate 17. Decorations and Medals

The War Order of the German Cross (30) in gold and silver versions was instituted in September 1941 and, as the actual badge was always worn no service ribbon of this award ever existed.

The Decoration of 9 November 1923 (31) also known as Blood Order, initially was awarded to those who participated in Hitler's first attempt to seize power, in 1923, but later it became a party decoration. No conventional service ribbon of the Blood Order ever existed.

The Life Saving Medal (32) was an old Prussian decoration revised by the Third Reich in 1937, while the Civil Defence Decoration (33) of 1st and 2nd Class was instituted in January 1938. Fire Brigade decorations existed long before 1936, when a national award was created (34). It was in two classes, the 1st Class was given for bravery and the 2nd for long service. An additional forty years' long service award of the 2nd Class was instituted in 1944. The Mine Rescue Service Decoration (35) was first instituted in 1936 and later modified in 1938.

As World War II was fatally approaching the German Defences Medal (36) came into being in August 1939 to reward those who were engaged in fortification works. Ribbons of this medal could be found with a bronze bar inscribed '1944'. In April of the same year a cross was given to the next-of-kin of Germans who had died in Spain (37) and, at the same time, a larger breast cross was created to commemorate direct participation in the Spanish Civil War.

The next few ribbons commemorate the events of pre-war German expansion, such as the annexion of Austria which took place on 13 March 1938 (38), the occupation of Czechoslovakia which started on 1 October 1938 (39), and the seizing of the Memel district from Lithuania in March 1939 (40). A clasp depicting Prague's castle could be worn on suspension and service ribbons of the second mentioned medal.

In May 1942 a medal was issued to all those who had taken part in the previous winter's campaign in Russia (41) while the campaign in North Africa (42) was commemorated by an Italian-made medal. The German version of its ribbon started with the black on the left while the Italian version started with the green. Further, the suspension ribbon of the former was 25 mm wide, and that of the latter 36 mm. (See Plate 37, ribbon No. 81.) The Bravery and Commemorative Medal of the Spanish Blue Division (43) was given to the personnel of this division fighting on the Russian front from 1941 to 1943.

The Mussert Cross (44) was a decoration of the Dutch Nazi Party, led by Anton Mussert from whom the award takes its name. Azad Hind means Free India (45) and this award was instituted by the Committee of Free India, created by the Germans during the war.

Decorations for Bravery and Meritorious Service for the Eastern People (46–48) were instituted in 1942 to reward Eastern Europeans who had taken arms on Germany's side. The gilt and silver awards of 1st Class were worn on the breast without a ribbon while the 2nd Class decoration in gilt, silver and bronze were worn like medals, each attached to a different ribbon. All could be awarded for bravery, with swords, or for meritorious service, without swords.

The Long Service Awards of the German National Socialist Party of the Workers (49–51) were instituted in 1939 in the form of crosses in gold, silver and bronze, with different ribbons. The centrepiece of the cross was in the form of a little badge in gold for twenty-five years of service, in silver for fifteen years and bronze for ten years, and was worn on the appropriate ribbons.

Mothers of large families were entitled to the Cross of Honour of the German Mother (52); in gilt for eight or more children, in silver for six or seven, and in bronze for four or five children.

Plate 18. Long Service Awards

Long service awards were distinguished by cornflower blue ribbons, with small badges on the service ribbons for the purpose of identification.

The Long Service Awards of the Armed Forces (53–56) were instituted in 1936 and an additional gold oak wreath was added on the ribbon of the twenty-five years' service award, in order to identify forty years of service. The award for twenty-five years of service was a gold cross and a silver cross for eighteen years. Medals in gold and silver were given for twelve and four years respectively. Personnel of the Army, Navy and Air Force wore a small metal replica of their breast badges, i.e. the eagle and swastika, on their service ribbons, as specified in the scheme below:

Silver Eagle	4 years of service
Gilt Eagle and Silver Eagle	12 years of service
Two Silver Eagles	18 years of service
Two Gold Eagles	25 years of service
Two Gold Eagles, the first one with a Gold Wreath	40 years of service

It should be noted that two ribbons were worn by all but those with four years of service.

The S.S. were entitled to four, eight, twelve and twenty-five years' Long Service Awards (57, 58), represented by black and bronze medals, a silver and a gold swastika respectively. A plain blue service ribbon was worn in the first case while a miniature replica of the bronze medal was attached to the service ribbons for eight years' service. Silver and gold S.S. runes on the ribbons identified awards for twelve and twenty-five years respectively.

Three Police Long Service Awards (59) existed from 1938, rewarding eight, twelve and twenty-five years of service: the service ribbon of the first was plain while the other two had additional silver or gold badges respectively. A late attempt to create a forty years' award was made in August 1944.

Customs officers and officials received their own award, in one class only, with the Customs' badge on the ribbon (60). The Faithful Service Decoration (61, 62) was given to the employees of public services for twenty-five and forty years of good performance. A special decoration was awarded for fifty years' service. Small replicas of the decorations were attached on to the service ribbons and only the latest award could be worn.

The Long Service Awards of the National Labour Service (63) were created in 1938 to reward four, twelve, eighteen and twenty-five years of service. German eagles, smaller than those of the armed forces, were worn on the service ribbons from November 1940 onwards. A different badge, the emblem of the Service (a spade and swastika on crossed wheatears) was adopted originally in August 1940.

Some Ribbons of the German States and Austria

Innumerable 15 mm ribbons can still be found: many belonged technically to the old German States, others were Austrian and others were foreign ribbons manufactured in Germany for the use of Germans who had been awarded foreign decorations. Only some examples of each type (65–74) have been illustrated, including that of the Cross of Danzig (70), a Nazi decoration in two classes, instituted in 1939.

Austrian servicemen fitted their German decorations with triangular-shaped ribbons (64), to match them with the decorations they had received before the Anschluss.

German Democratic Republic

Plate 19. Orders and Medals

The Order of Karl Marx (1) was created in 1953, on the 70th anniversary of his death, as a reward for outstanding contributions in the fields of science, art and culture, and German national economy. It is awarded in one class only, consisting of a gold and red enamel badge suspended on a red crossed ribbon: a gold oak leaf is worn on the service ribbon of the order.

The Order of Merit of the Fatherland (2, 3), instituted in 1954, is divided into three classes with gold, silver and bronze badges respectively attached to an unusual suspension, as illustrated. This suspension, a ribbon above stylised oak leaves, on its own, is the service ribbon of the order.

General Gerhard Johann David von Scharnhorst was the main organiser of the liberation struggle of 1813–15 against French rule and the highest military award is dedicated to his patriotism: the Scharnhorst Order (4). The Order of the Banner of Work (5, 6) was instituted in 1954 as a reward for individuals or collectives who have excelled in promoting national production. The badge depicts the emblem of the G.D.R. below a red flying banner and its ribbon, crossed in the usual fashion, is half red and the other half, on the right, is black, red and yellow, the national colours. The original ribbon has now been substituted by another one, with a gold badge in its centre instead of the national colours.

The Field-Order of Merit for the People and Fatherland (7) is another purely military award, in three classes, gold, silver and bronze, identified on the service ribbon by crossed swords of corresponding metals.

The Order of the Star of Friendship between Peoples (8) was founded in 1959 and consists of a Grand Star, a Gold Star and a Silver Star, which are awarded for achievements in promoting peace and international friendship. A sash ribbon, red edged with the German colours, is worn by recipients of the Grand Star.

The National People's Army Meritorious Medal (9) and the Brotherhood-under-Arms Medal (10) both are awarded in gold, silver and bronze. A bronze medal only is awarded for Exceptional Border Service to the Border Guards of the G.D.R. (11). The National People's Army Faithful Service Medal (12) is a long service award in four classes, distinguished by Roman numbers on both the suspension and the service ribbons.

The military academy of the N.P.A. is named after Frederick Engels, the nineteenth century prophet of Communism, and also gold, silver and bronze Prize Medals (13) are given in his name. The medals depict Engels' face and a miniature replica of the medal is worn on the service ribbon. Theodore Körner was a soldier and poet who fought in the National War of 1813–15, and to him a modern silver Prize Medal (14) is dedicated. The National Emblem of the G.D.R. is attached to its service ribbon.

German Federal Republic

Plate 20. Orders and Decorations

The Order of Merit of the German Federal Republic (1) was instituted in September 1951 in response to the necessity of possessing a national award for the benefit of eligible Germans and foreigners alike. The order is divided into eight classes as follows:

Special Class of the Grand Cross of Merit (4) with the Cross, or Badge of the order on a sash and the Star (eight-pointed) of the order on the breast.

Grand Cross of Merit (5), with the Cross on a sash and the Star (six-pointed).

Grand Cross of Merit of Special Design, with the same insignia as above but with additional laurel wreath behind the centre of the crosses.

Grand Cross of Merit with Star and sash (6), with the Cross on a sash and the Star (four-pointed).

Grand Cross of Merit with Star (7), with the Cross on a neck ribbon and a square-shaped Star.

Grand Cross of Merit (8, 9), with a neck Cross only.

Cross of Merit 1st Class (10), with a pin-back breast Cross.

Cross of Merit on Ribbon (11, 12), with the Cross worn suspended by a straight ribbon, like a medal.

The buttonhole ribbons of this order have been illustrated and, in two cases, the bows worn by ladies. A soldier would wear the same miniature badges, the first four representing the stars of the order, on a service ribbon (2) 40 mm in width down to the Grand Cross of Merit, and 25 mm ribbon for the lower classes.

A Medal of Merit (13) is affiliated to the order; it depicts the cross and the eagle in red and black enamel mounted on a circular medal. A different ribbon identifies this medal (3).

The Ordre Pour le Mérite for Science and the Arts (14) was re-instituted in 1952. Originally instituted in 1842 it was abolished by the 1930s. The insignia, of one class only, is worn on a neck ribbon.

Following a tradition introduced by the German States before Unification, gold and silver Mine Rescue Decorations (15, 16) were re-instated in July 1953, with gold and silver edges on their ribbons respectively. The German Red Cross Decorations, in gold and silver classes (17, 18), also reappeared in 1953. These are plain crosses of white enamel with a red cross in the centre surrounded by a round laurel wreath of metal; both are suspended on a ribbon edged in gold or silver respectively. The ribbon of the Life Saving Medal (19) has remained the same as usual while a new ribbon has been granted for merit in the field of sports (20). A small replica of the actual badge, the Sportabzeichen, which could be in gold, silver or bronze is worn on the ribbon. The initials D.S.B. stand for Deutsche Sports Bund.

Plate 21. Decorations and Medals

From 1945 to 1957 the use of war-time decorations and badges was forbidden but since then permission has been given to wear the old decorations but in a modified form. Nazi eagles, swastikas and similar party emblems have been removed and in certain cases the wearing of some awards has been changed altogether.

As all breast pocket badges have been abolished the corresponding awards are now worn on ribbons, even in the case of the Iron Cross, the 1st Class of which is now identified by a miniature replica of the cross on the service ribbon of the 2nd Class (28, 29). A slightly larger badge, on a wider ribbon (40 mm) identifies the holder of a Knight's Cross (21). The three oak leaves of the 1813 pattern have replaced the swastika of the war-time cross (27). As the diagonal buttonhole ribbons have been abolished, the Clasps of Honour in reduced and denazified form are now worn on service ribbons (22–24) as well.

The insignia of the Order of the German Cross have been entirely modified: the gold badge now bears the Iron Cross in its centre (25), and the silver one has the War Merit Cross in its centre, in place of the swastika (26). Service ribbons are now worn as well. The War Merit Cross (30–33) did not change greatly, except that the date '1939' previously on the reverse, now substitutes the swastika on the obverse.

The war-time breast pocket badges were awarded as decorations and therefore since 1957 have been placed in miniature form on ribbons (34–37), including the Single-Handed Tank Destruction Badge (38) previously worn on the upper sleeve and the Wound Badge (39), previously a breast insignia. Former cuff titles have been transformed into service ribbons (40, 41) and the swastika has been omitted from the Long Service Awards of the Armed Forces (42, 43).

Many other ribbons, with different badges, exist as well; only a representative selection of the modern German ribbons have been illustrated because, obviously, no war medals have been awarded since 1945 and, in the meantime, the few war veterans who joined the new army are now retired. Therefore these new ribbons are very seldom worn.

Great Britain

Plate 22. Victoria and George Cross, and Orders of Knighthood
The structure of the awards of many nations has changed after lost wars or revolutions but, as nothing of this nature has happened to the United Kingdom in centuries, the ancient orders of knighthood are still in existence and innumerable decorations and medals have been created in the meantime.

Mammoth books have been written on this subject and should be consulted by those especially interested in British awards; the scope of this book is to provide information on the ribbons of many nations and the size allows me to write only the minimum that is indispensable on the 313 ribbons and medals illustrated in this section.

Strict regulations rule the wearing of British awards: I have tried my best to draw these ribbons following the correct order of precedence and group them into separate sections, and plates, at the same time. At times this compromise just could not be attained.

The classes of the British orders of knighthood are not identified by rosettes or any other devices on the service ribbon, but the plain ribbon alone is worn on the breast. Badges and devices used are described in this text.

The Victoria Cross (1-3) and the George Cross (4) are the highest British decorations and their ribbons precede those of the orders of Knighthood. The former was instituted by Queen Victoria in 1856 and, until World I, the naval decoration was suspended by blue ribbon (2). A miniature replica of the cross is attached to the service ribbon worn on undress uniform (1). The George Cross was founded in 1941 as a replacement for the Medal for Gallantry of the Order of the British Empire and rewards, primarily, civilian gallantry, contrary to the Victoria Cross, which is a military decoration. A small replica of the George Cross is worn on its service ribbon (4).

There is no service ribbon for the Order of the Garter (5), the Order of the Thistle (6), the Order of St Patrick (7), nor for the Royal Guelphic Order (15) and therefore the sash ribbons of the first three orders have been illustrated in their place, plus the insignia of the latter.

The Most Noble Order of the Garter dates back to 1348 and was created by King Edward III. The Most Noble and Most Ancient Order of the Thistle is supposed to trace its origins to 787, was reinstated by James II in 1687, and later by Queen Anne, in 1703. The Most Illustrious Order of St Patrick was instituted by George III in 1783. Due to their unbroken traditions, these orders are not divided into classes but consist of the Sovereign and a number of knights.

The Most Honourable Order of the Bath (8) initially was created in 1399 and updated by George I in 1725. Until 1847 it was strictly a military order but in that year a Civil Division of the order was instituted also. Both divisions are divided into three classes: Knight of Grand Cross (G.C.B.), Knight Commander (K.C.B.) and Companion (C.B.). The recipients of any class of this order wear the same ribbon in undress uniform.

The Order of Merit (9) was created in 1902, in one class, with crossed swords on the insignia for military men and without swords for civilians. The Most Exalted Order of the Star of India (10) was instituted in 1861 in three classes: Knight Grand Commander (G.C.S.I.), Knight Commander (K.C.S.I.) and Companion (C.S.I.); all wear the same service ribbon.

The Most Distinguished Order of St Michael and St George (11) was founded by George III in 1818 and includes Knights of Grand Cross (G.C.M.G.), Knights Commanders (K.C.M.G.) and Companions (C.M.G.). The Most Eminent Order of the Indian Empire (12) founded in 1878 has the usual three classes but Knight Grand Commander (G.C.I.E.) is the title of the 1st Class. The Royal Victorian Order (13) was created in 1896 to reward valuable services to the Sovereign and the Royal Family and can also be bestowed upon ladies. It has five classes: Knight, or Dame, of Grand Cross (G.C.V.O.), Knight, or Dame, Commander (K.C.V.O. or D.C.V.O.), Commanders (C.V.O.) and Members of the 4th and of the 5th Class (M.V.O.). Medals in gilt, silver and bronze also are affiliated to this order and those awarded to foreigners have a narrow red stripe in the centre of the ribbon.

The Order of the Companions of Honour (14) rewards men and women who have rendered conspicuous service of national importance. There is only one class and foreign citizens may be appointed as honorary members. The Order was founded by George V in 1917. The ribbon is carmine with borders of gold thread. The Royal Guelphic Order (15) was founded in 1815 and became obsolete after the 1830s.

The Distinguished Service Order (16) was established in 1886 to reward distinguished service by officers who have been specially recommended in Despatches for service in the field. Clasps are awarded for succeeding acts of gallantry, and each clasp is shown on the service ribbon by a Silver Rose.

Plate 23. Orders and Decorations
The Most Excellent Order of the British Empire (O.B.E.) (17–21) was instituted in 1917 primarily as a civilian award, although officers of the services could be eligible for non-combatant merits. The Military Division of this order was created in 1918. Both divisions have five classes, as follows: Knight Grand Cross (G.B.E.), Knight Commander (K.B.E.), Commander (C.B.E.), Officer (O.B.E.) and Member (M.B.E.). Ladies can be appointed to the order as well. Until 1936 the ribbons of the order were crimson, that of the Military Division had a red stripe in the centre (17, 18), later the ribbons were changed to rose-pink with grey edges, that of the Military Division with a grey stripe in the centre as well (19–21).

The Imperial Service Order and Medal (22) were instituted in 1902 to reward long meritorious service although meritorious acts could be considered as well. Long and faithful service of native officers was rewarded by the Order of British India (23–27) instituted in 1837. Its light blue ribbon was changed to crimson the year after the ribbon of the 1st Class, for officers, measured 50 mm in width, while that of the 2nd Class, for N.C.O.s, measure 38 mm only (24, 25). Amendments made in 1941 added blue stripes on both ribbons (26, 27). The Indian Order of Merit (28, 29) was also instituted in 1837 but as a gallantry award, originally in three classes, all using the same service ribbon. The highest class was abolished in 1912 and the order as a whole was modified during World War II when also a Civil Division was instituted, of one class only.

The Baronet's Badge (30) has a long history that goes back to 1629 but was revived only in 1929 and does not grant the use of a service ribbon.

The Kaisar-I-Hind Medal (31) in gold, silver and bronze was the last decoration created by Queen Victoria, in 1900. The medals could be given to any person, regardless of race, sex or occupation, who had rendered eminent services towards the advancement and benefit of India. Its original ribbon was light blue but later darker ribbons were issued. The Order of Burma (32) was instituted in 1940 as a long service award for officers of the Burma Army, Frontier Force and Military Police; the Burma Gallantry Medal (43) was instituted on the same date.

In 1883 Queen Victoria instituted the Royal Red Cross Decorations (33) as a reward for ladies or nursing sisters only. Recipients of the 1st Class are designated Members, those of the 2nd Class are Associates.

Edward VII instituted the Conspicuous Service Cross in 1901 as a naval decoration which rewards warrant officers and subordinate officers for 'Meritorious or distinguished service before the enemy'. The decoration was renamed Distinguished Service Cross (34) in 1914 and in 1939 officers up to the rank of Commander became eligible to receive it. The Military Cross (35) was instituted in 1914 and is conferred on warrant officers and officers up to the rank of major for 'gallant and distinguished services in action' (Amendment of 1931). Succeeding awards are identified by bars on the suspension ribbon and Silver Roses on the service ribbon. R.A.F. officers and warrant officers can receive it for deeds performed on the ground. Their acts of gallantry performed against the enemy while on flying duty are rewarded by the Distinguished Flying Cross (38, 39) instituted in 1918. The Air Force Cross (40, 41) was also created in 1918 and is awarded on the same conditions, though not for active operations.

The Navy Conspicuous Gallantry Medal (36, 37), the Royal Air Force Conspicuous Gallantry Medal (42) and the Distinguished Conduct Medal of the Army (44) are all for petty officers, non-commissioned officers and men of the services. The former was instituted during the Crimean War and revived in 1874. Its original ribbon was changed in 1921 for that of the Naval General Service Medal 1793-1840. The R.A.F. award was instituted in 1943, while the Medal for Distinguished Conduct in the Field (D.C.M.) was created in 1854: second and succeeding awards are shown on the service ribbon by Silver Roses. In 1903 a similar medal was granted to the natives of the West African Frontier Force and later it became the Royal West African Frontier Force/King's African Rifles Distinguished Conduct Medal (45).

The Navy Distinguished Service Medal (46) was established in October 1914 and although a bravery award for petty officers and men, it rewards lesser acts of courage than are required for the Conspicuous

Gallantry Medal. The Indian Distinguished Service Medal (47) was already in existence in 1907 to reward all native ranks of the Indian Army.

Plate 24. Orders, Decorations and Medals

The George Medal (48) was instituted in 1940 to be awarded in circumstances similar to those required for the George Cross, but of lesser merit. The Silver Rose on service ribbons identify, as usual, a second award. The Edward Medal (49) in silver or in bronze, is a reward for individuals who at the risk of their own life endeavour to save someone else's life in mines, quarries or in some industrial activity. It is now a posthumous award only.

The Military Medal (50) is given to warrant officers, N.C.O.s and men for bravery in the field; it was created in 1916. The Distinguished Flying Medal (52, 53) and the Air Force Medal (54, 55) are both awarded to N.C.O.s and men on the same conditions as the respective officers' crosses. Their ribbons, violet and white, and crimson and white, have been changed from horizontal alternate stripes to diagonal stripes.

The Constabulary Medal of Ireland (51) was a reward of merit and its green ribbon should have been placed among the other police medals illustrated below. However, it is placed after the Military Medal only in order to balance the ribbons which follow in the same plate.

The Most Venerable Order of the Hospital of St John of Jerusalem (56–59) is an ancient order of mercy which traces its origins to a hospital founded in about 1070 by Italian merchants in Jerusalem. It became a religious order of Chivalry and when Jerusalem was lost in 1291 it moved to Cyprus, to Rhodes and eventually to Malta where it stayed until Napoleon occupied the island in 1798. Finally, in the 1820s, the order moved to Rome. It has branches all over Europe and in England since 1888. Initially its members were divided into knights (engaged in checking the spread of Turkish rule in the Mediterranean), priests and lay brothers for hospital work.

The ribbons of the British Empire Medal (60–63) have the same colours as those of the order although they measure 32 mm instead of 38 mm in width. The medal was instituted in 1917 and a Military Division of the award was added the year after. In 1922 a Medal for Gallantry and a Medal for Meritorious Service, both Civil and Military Divisions, replaced the previous pattern but in 1940 the Gallantry Medal was superseded by the George Cross. Succeeding awards of the British Empire Medal for Meritorious Service are identified by Silver Roses on the service ribbon, while Silver Crossed Oak Leaves on the ribbon, since 1958 identify appointment to, or promotion in the Order of the British Empire and awards of the medal, granted for gallantry.

The King's Police Medal was instituted in July 1909 as a reward for officers of the police and fire brigade serving in the United Kingdom and Dominions. Its ribbon was dark blue with white side stripes, and a central white stripe was added in 1916 and, in 1933, this award branched into a King's Police Distinguished Service Medal (64) and the King's Police Gallantry Medal (65), the latter with additional narrow red stripes within the white stripes of the old ribbon. These medals continued to be awarded to officers of the fire brigades as well and in 1940 they were retitled Police and Fire Brigade Medals, until 1954 when the Queen's Fire Service Medal for Distinguished Service and for Gallantry (66, 67) were instituted.

The Indian Police Medal was created in 1932 for Distinguished Conduct (68) and another award was later instituted for Gallantry (69). Colonial Police medals were instituted during the reign of Queen Victoria and in 1934 Colonial Police and Fire Brigade medals were created by George V. In 1938 a number of such medals were instituted, namely the Colonial Police Gallantry Medal, and for Meritorious Service and medals of the Colonial Fire Brigades, the ribbons of which are illustrated in Plate 30. The Special Constabulary Faithful Service Medal (70) came in 1918 to reward the World War I service of volunteers of the Special Constabulary and continued to be awarded in the following years.

There are four classes of the Hong Kong Police Force Medal for Merit (72-75): the medal of 1st Class is made of gold, the 2nd Class in silver and the other two medals are of bronze, and all have different ribbons.

The Union of South Africa King's (later Queen's) Medal for Bravery (76) is a civilian life saving award adopted in 1939. The Canadian Forces Decoration (78) was instituted in 1951 as a reward for officers and men who have served for twelve years on the active or reserve list of the armed forces.

Polar Medals (79) have been awarded since 1857 and are still issued, when applicable, over a century later: they commemorate successive Arctic and Antarctic expeditions and the usual Rose can be worn on the ribbon to denote second and further awards.

Plate 25. War Medals

The first war medals were issued on the occasion of Lord Howe's naval victory over the French on 1 June 1794; these gold medals were awarded in two sizes, 50 mm and 32 mm and were worn with a 44 mm ribbon, around the neck and at the buttonhole by admirals and captains respectively. These medals continued to be issued by the Admiralty in the event of famous battles until 1815 (80).

In 1808 a gold medal was granted to thirteen officers as a reward for the victory at Maida (85), in Calabria, two years earlier. Later other officers obtained some large and small gold medals and a cross for their participation in the Peninsula Campaign against the French (81). However, as only one medal could be worn from 1813 onwards, a large decorated clasp was attached to its suspension ribbon for each successive engagement. All the above medals were awarded to senior ranking officers while the Waterloo Medal (86) was given to all those who took part in the battle, regardless of rank.

The distinctive colours of the ribbons of these first medals, white and blue and crimson and blue, in 1847 were selected for the ribbons of the Naval General Service Medal 1793–1840 (82) and Military General Service 1793–1814 (83) of the army respectively.

The Seringapatam Medal (84) was issued by the Honourable East India Company in gold, silver-gilt, silver, bronze and tin variations to all ranks who had taken part in the capture of Seringapatam in 1799. In 1826 the Company awarded another medal for the First Burmese War 1824–26 (87) and in 1851 yet another one, which commemorates general service in India, known as the Army of India Medal 1799–1826 (88). It carries engagement clasps on its suspension ribbon.

The capture of the fortress of Ghuznee took place in 1839 during the First Afghan War; the Ghuznee Medal (89) was intended to hang from a yellow and green ribbon while a yellow and crimson ribbon was manufactured instead. The ribbon of the Jellalabad Medal (90) suggests the colours of the eastern sunrise: the medal was awarded to all those who took part in the defence of Jellalabad and the same ribbon was used later for the Kelat-I-Ghilzie Medal which commemorates another defensive battle, the Scinde Medal, the Gwalior Campaign Stars and the Kabul to Kandahar Star of 1880.

The first China Medal (91) commemorates operations that took place in 1840–42 while in 1857–60 a second expedition was mounted and medals were issued of which two patterns of ribbon have been illustrated (102, 103). A third expedition took place in 1900 (Plate 26, 127) against the 'Boxers' and was formed by military contingents of various nationalities.

The next medal commemorates the Sutlej Campaign 1845–46 (92) of the Sikh War and in 1869 a medal was instituted to reward all ranks who took part in the 1845–47 and 1860–66 war against the Maoris, in New Zealand (93). In 1848–49 another campaign against the Sikhs led to the annexion of the Punjab and a medal was issued accordingly (94). The India General Service Medal, issued in 1854 (96), covers the Burmah Campaign 1853–54 with additional clasps for operations taking place until 1894–95.

A General Order of 1854 created the South Africa Medal (95) for the wars of 1835–36, 1846–47 and 1850–53, and another medal but with the same ribbon was issued later for the 1877–79 campaign.

The Crimea War was fought by Turkey, Britain, France and the Kingdom of Sardinia against Russia in the years 1854–56 (98) and, the same war led to the creation of the Baltic Medal (97) which commemorates the blockade of the Baltic. A considerable exchanging of decorations took place amongst the allies and two ribbons of foreign medals awarded to British servicemen have been illustrated (99, 100).

The Indian Mutiny Medal 1857–58 (101) was the last one given by the Honourable East India Company in the name of the British Government; clasps were attached to its suspension ribbon. The Canada General Service Medal (104) was authorised in 1899 retrospective to service from 1866 to 1870. The 1867–68 Expedition in Abyssinia (105) is commemorated by a medal with a dark red and white ribbon while a yellow ribbon with black stripes identifies the 1873–74 campaign in Ashantee (106) and successive campaigns on that continent. It should not be confused with the ribbon of the Africa General Service (Plate 26, 132) which has narrow green stripes in its centre.

Another silver medal was awarded for the Afghanistan War of 1878–80 (107) and the Cape of Good Hope General Service Medal (108) was issued in 1900 to colonial troops who had served between 1880 and 1897 in the regions defined on the attached clasps.

Plate 26. War Medals

The remaining colonial campaigns, up to World War I, are commemorated by the ribbons illustrated in this plate.

The 1882–89 operations in Egypt and in the Sudan are remembered by a silver medal (109) and by a bronze star (110), the latter awarded by the Khedive of Egypt. The North West Canada Medal (111) was issued to troops taking part in the quelling of the 1885 rebellion.

The next ribbon refers to a medal issued by the Royal Niger Company in 1899 for participation in punitive expeditions during the period 1886–97 (112); the British South Africa Company also issued medals the last of which was awarded in 1927 (113). The Central Africa Medal (114) was issued in two variations, to commemorate a number of campaigns fought from 1891 to 1898.

A new India General Service Medal (115) was instituted in 1896 to commemorate the Chitral Campaign of 1895 and other military events up to the Waziristan Campaign 1901–02. The Maharajah of Kashmir awarded a different medal for the defence and relief of Chitral (116).

The Ashanti Star (117) was granted for the 1895–96 Ashanti Expedition and the Queen's Sudan Medal (118) commemorates Lord Kitchener's campaign of 1896–98. The Khedive of Egypt instituted a medal also, with clasps dated until 1908 (119).

Four different ribbons were manufactured for the medals of the British North Borneo Company: the orange ribbon is a first pattern worn with the punitive expeditions medals, later changed to the second pattern (120, 121). The Tambunan Expedition Medal (124) had a half green and half orange ribbon while the Company's General Service Medal (123) was attached to a ribbon with the same colours in three stripes.

A half yellow and half red ribbon identifies the East and Central Africa Medal (122) related to operations that took place in Uganda in the years 1897–99. The Ashanti Medal (128) rewarded the troops which suppressed the 1900 native revolt in that region.

The Anglo-Boer War gave birth to a number of medals, starting with the well-known Queen's and King's South Africa Medals (125, 129) and the Kimberley Star (126), awarded by the Mayor of Kimberley to the defenders of that town. The Transport Medal (130) was awarded to personnel of the Mercantile Marine engaged in ferrying troops and supplies to South Africa, and to China during the 'Boxers' revolt. The Cape Copper Company gave a medal to those who took part in the defence of mines in South West Africa during that conflict (131). In 1920 the South African Government instituted two medals and a Wound Ribbon without medal (133–135) for Boers who had taken part in the previous war.

The Tibet Medal (136) commemorates the military operations which took place between December 1903 and September 1904 in Tibet. In 1908 a medal was issued to those who took part in the quelling of the 1906 Zulu rebellion; it is also known as the Natal Medal (137). The India General Service Medals (138) bear the effigies of Edward VII and George V and reward military operations extended until 1935. It was superseded by another medal in 1936 (Plate 27, 149). The Naval General Service Medal (141) was instituted in 1915 and its first clasp refers to operations in the Persian Gulf, between 1909 and 1914.

The 1914 Star (140) was instituted in 1917 and a clasp (bar) inscribed '5th Aug.–22nd Nov. 1914' was granted in 1919; a White Rose on the service ribbon identifies the holder of the bar. A similar bronze star, but with the dates '1914–1915' in the centre, was granted in 1918 and is suspended by the ribbon of the previous star. A special medal was created in 1922 to reward French and Belgian civilians who aided British prisoners of war (142).

Plate 27. War Medals

A commemorative medal of World War I (143) was instituted in 1919 and its eligibility was extended for post-war operations in the Baltic, Serbia and Russia. The Territorial Force War Medal (144) was adopted in 1920 as a reward for territorials who served for at least four years in the force and had volunteered for overseas service on, or before 30 September 1914. The Mercantile Marine War Medal (145) was awarded to personnel who served at sea for a period of at least six months during World War I.

The Gallipoli Star (146) should have been awarded to Australians and New Zealanders who took part in that expedition but this project never materialised, as it would have been unfair to the British and Indian troops who also landed at Gallipoli. The Victory Medal (148) closes the series of World War I awards; a Spray of Oak leaves in bronze was attached to the ribbons of individuals who had been mentioned in despatches by a commander-in-chief in the field.

The General Service Medal (147) for the Army and R.A.F. was instituted in 1918 and later the India General Service Medal (149) and the Sudan General Service Medal (150) were adopted in 1936 and in 1933 respectively.

Some eight six-pointed stars with different ribbons, were created to reward active service during World War II and rather complicated rules regulated their concession. In brief, the 1939–45 Star (151) was given for a determinate period of service between 3 September 1939 and 15 August 1945. The colours of its ribbon stand for the Royal Navy, the Army and the R.A.F. and a Gilt Rose on the service ribbon identified service as air crew of fighter aircraft during the Battle of Britain. The Africa Star (152) was awarded for service in North and East Africa from 10 June 1940 to 12 May 1943; metal numbers '1' and '8' on the service ribbons identify personnel of the First and Eighth Armies (153) respectively. In particular circumstances the Silver Rose can be worn as well, but only one device, a number or the rose, can be worn on the same ribbon.

The Air Crew Europe Star (154) rewarded operational flights over Europe from bases in Britain and individuals who qualified also for other stars, such as the Atlantic Star or the France and Germany Star, or both. Only the one earned first was worn, with a clasp on the suspension ribbon and the Silver Rose on the service ribbon. Only one clasp and one rose could be considered. The France and Germany Star (155) was awarded for service from 6 June 1944 in Normandy to the end of the war; a Silver Rose could be worn on the service ribbon on the same conditions described above. The Atlantic Star (156) commemorates the Battle of the Atlantic and was awarded to personnel of the Royal Navy, Merchant Navy, R.A.F. and also to Army personnel taking part in active operations afloat. A Silver Rose could be worn, as mentioned above.

The Pacific Star (157) was granted for service in that operational area from 8 December 1941 and 2 September 1945. Individuals entitled to the Pacific Star and the Burma Star can wear only the first one gained, with a clasp, and a Silver Rose on the ribbons to identify the second star. The Italy Star (158) was awarded in addition to any others previously received. The Burma Star (159) rewards service from 11 December 1941 and a Silver Rose on its ribbon identified the subsequent eligibility to the Pacific Star as well.

The Defence Medal (160) was basically awarded for three years of service in the United Kingdom or one year overseas, however in certain conditions the necessary period for qualification could be reduced to six months, or even three months in the specific case of personnel of Mine and Bomb Disposal units. Many rules regulate the awarding of this medal and exceed the scope of this book which is primarily concerned with service ribbons. A Silver Laurel Leaves emblem is worn on the ribbon to identify a King's commendation for brave conduct for civilians. The War Medal 1939–45 (161) required the qualification of twenty-eight days of operational and non-operational service. An emblem, depicting a single bronze oak leaf could be worn on the suspension and service ribbons by individuals mentioned in despatches. The same emblem was also worn by those mentioned in despatches for operational service in the period between the two world wars, from 1920 to 1939 and after 1945. The bronze leaf can be worn on the ribbon of the Naval General Service Medal 1915, the General Service Medal 1918 or the India General Service Medal. The King's Commendation for brave conduct, or for valuable service in the air is also represented by the same emblem, but only one emblem can be worn on a ribbon. If the recipient of mention in despatch or a commendation is not eligible for the appropriate medal he should attach the emblem, on its own, after all the other ribbons, or in place of the first ribbon if he has not got any at all.

The Canada Medal (162) was instituted in 1943 to reward meritorious service 'above and beyond the faithful performance of duties', while the Canadian Volunteer Service Medal (163) was awarded to volunteers who had at least eighteen months of good service. Australia, New Zealand, South Africa and Southern Rhodesia issued war service medals as well (164–168); the Africa Service Medal (166) was for armed forces personnel who fought the enemy, on African territory, until May 1943, while the Medal for War Service (167) was given to civilians for their contribution to the war effort.

The India General Service Medal 1939–45 (169) was awarded for three years of non-operational service and in 1955 a new Africa General Service Medal was adopted, with the same ribbon as that of the Africa General Service Medal, adopted in 1902.

In 1949 a medal was instituted to commemorate the Independence of India (170); the India Police Independence Medal (171) and the Pakistan Independence Medal (172) followed as also medals to celebrate the independence of other new nations. The British Medal for Korea (173) was instituted in 1951 and should not be confused with the United Nations Service Medal (174) created in the same year, which was awarded by the United Nations Organisation. A United Nations Medal was also awarded for service in Cyprus (175). A Malaya Medal was issued after Independence (176). A new General Service Medal (177) was adopted in 1962 and the Vietnam Medal (178) later was awarded to Australian servicemen who participated in that war.

Plate 28. Coronation, Jubilee Medals, Royal Household Ribbons, etc.

The Badge of Honour (179) was a decoration for native dignitaries of the colonies which was worn suspended around the neck by a 38 mm ribbon or on the breast, as a medal, attached to a conventional ribbon 32 mm in width.

The Empress of India Medal (180), in gold or silver, was also attached to a neck ribbon, 44 mm wide, but could not be worn by its recipients on military uniform. The medals commemorate Queen Victoria's investiture as Empress of India, which took place at Delhi in 1877.

Special medals of gold, silver and bronze were struck to commemorate Queen Victoria's Jubilee in 1887 (1837-87) and her Diamond Jubilee in 1897 (181) and were all attached to the same ribbon. However, different medals with a different ribbon were given to civilian personages (182) and other medals to policemen (183) who took part in the ceremonies. The dark blue ribbon of the latter was used again in 1900 with another police medal commemorating the Queen's visit to Ireland.

The coronation of Edward VII, on 26 June 1902, is remembered by silver and bronze medals (184) with affiliated variations for civilians (185) and policemen (186) in attendance. The following year the King visited Scotland (187), Ireland (188) and India and medals were struck on each occasion. The Delhi Durbar Medal (189) was issued in gold, silver and bronze.

George V ascended the throne in 1911 and a medal was issued for his coronation (190); the same ribbon was used for the medal of George V's Delhi Durbar of 1911 during which the Title Badges (194-196) were awarded to civilians and officers of the Indian Army. Some Police Coronation Medals (191) were issued as well, with different denominations on the reverse but all attached to the same ribbon. Different medals commemorate the King's visit to Ireland (192) in 1911 and the Silver Jubilee of his reign (193), in 1935.

Medals were struck to commemorate the coronation of George VI in 1937 (197) and Elizabeth II in 1953 (197, 199). The medals for ladies, as usual, are attached to a bow as illustrated (198).

The King Edward VII's Medal for Science, Art and Music (200) was awarded between 1902 and 1906 only.

Family Orders have been instituted by succeeding sovereigns who bestow them upon female relatives or, sometimes, upon ladies as a token of esteem and favour. They consist of badges in precious metals and stones attached to bows of silk ribbon. In more modern times, in 1862, Queen Victoria instituted the Royal Order of Victoria and Albert, the badges of which were attached to white moiré ribbon, 38 mm in width. Edward VII created his own Royal Family Order in 1902 (202) and the successive sovereigns followed the same custom. The ribbons of the Family Orders of King George V and King George VI were light blue and light crimson respectively, both 50 mm wide. The ribbon of the Royal Family Order of Queen Elizabeth II is Chartreuse yellow, also 50 mm in width. Ladies in Attendance had badges of office also attached to bows of ribbon (201, 204, 205). Of course there are no service ribbons of these special orders.

Plate 29. Meritorious Service, Long Service and Good Conduct Medals and Territorial Decorations.

Originally, twenty-one years of good service were the required qualification for receiving the naval Long Service and Good Conduct Medal, an award for petty officers and seamen of equivalent ranks of the Royal Marines. The medal was instituted in 1831 by William IV and was attached to a dark blue ribbon 25 mm wide (206) which was changed to a wider pattern, with white edges in 1848 (207). It is now awarded for fifteen years of irreproachable service and recipients of a second award are entitled to a clasp on the suspension ribbon and wear a silver rosette on the service ribbon.

The Army Long Service and Good Conduct Medal was created in 1833 as a modification of a similar decoration instituted in November 1829 (208). The colours of its ribbon were modified in 1915.

The Army Meritorious Service Medal (209), instituted in 1845 was also attached to a crimson ribbon while the Royal Marines Meritorious Service Medal (212) was created four years later and was in practice the same medal with a different ribbon. The ribbon of the former was changed in 1915 (209) and in 1919 also the Royal Marines adopted the same ribbon (213).

A Meritorious Service Medal similar to that of the Army was awarded also to petty officers and seamen from 1919 to 1928 and an airmen's version of this award was introduced in 1919 (221).

This is also an other rank's award and it is given for distinguished and valuable service other than in action, irrespective of service length.

Following the example of the major services, Long Service and Good Conduct Medals were adopted by the Royal Naval Reserve and Royal Naval Auxiliary Service (210, 211, 218), by the Royal Naval Volunteer Reserve (215) and by the Special Reserve (219) around the years 1908–10. The Special Reserve Medal substituted the Long Service Medal of the former Militia (216) which together with the Imperial Yeomanry Long Service Medal, existed from 1904 to 1908. The Royal Air Force Long Service and Good Conduct Medal (217) was instituted in 1919 and the

Royal Fleet Reserve (214) adopted its own award in 1930.

Long service and meritorious medals were awarded all over the Commonwealth to members of the military forces, police and fire brigades and more of their ribbons have been illustrated in the following plate. At this point, however, it is necessary to continue examining the awards adopted in the British Isles.

The Volunteer Officers' Decoration (222) rewards long and meritorious service by officers and was instituted by Queen Victoria in 1892; its use was extended to India and the colonies two years later. In the same year a similar award was instituted for the other ranks of the Volunteer Force and was extended to India and the colonies in 1896. The ribbons of both were deep green, that of the decoration was 38 mm in width while that of the medal, the latter described, was only 32 mm wide, like the first pattern of the Royal Naval Reserve's ribbon (210).

In 1908 the Volunteer Force was superseded by the Territorial Force and in consequence these awards had to be modified and the Territorial Decoration (223) and Efficiency Medal (226) were adopted as a result. The latter in turn were replaced in 1930 by the Efficiency Decoration and Efficiency Medal, and a different ribbon, with yellow edges (227) was adopted for the medal.

Decorations and medals awarded to members of the Honourable Artillery Company were attached to a different ribbon, 38 mm or 32 mm wide, inspired by the racing colours of Edward VII (224, 225). Following the raising of the Army Emergency Reserve a decoration for officers and a medal for the other ranks were adopted in 1952 (228, 229), while the Civil Defence Medal (236) and the Women's Voluntary Services Medal (237) were authorised in 1961. The latter two medals are granted after fifteen years' service and the reverse of the Civil Defence Medal bears the initials of the Civil Defence, of the Auxiliary Fire Service and of the National Hospital Service Reserve on appropriate shields.

The Royal Naval Reserve (230) and Volunteer Reserve (231) Decorations were established in 1910 as the officer's counterpart of the Royal Naval Reserve and Volunteer Reserve Medals, already described. The Royal Naval Reserve Decoration was attached to a plain green 38 mm ribbon until 1941 when white stripes were added to its edges; the ribbon of the Royal Naval Volunteer Reserve Decoration, initially also green, was altered in 1922, to the type illustrated (231).

The Naval Engineers' Ability and Good Conduct Medal (238) was instituted in 1842 but only seven awards were ever made: its ribbon was 42 mm in width. The Naval Good Shooting Medal (232) rewarded good performance by gunners during target practice between 1903 and 1914.

George VI instituted the Air Efficiency Award (233) in August 1942 for the benefit of officers and men of the Auxiliary Air Force and Royal Air Force Volunteer Reserve of Britain and the Commonwealth. The

Sudan decoration and medal were both instituted in 1933 as a reward for eighteen years' service.

Plate 30. Meritorious Service, and Long Service and Good Conduct Medals

By the beginning of this century long service medals were adopted by the armed forces of many dominions and colonies. The Royal West African Frontier Force and the King's African Rifles had their own individual medals with the same ribbon (241) granted in 1903 and 1907 respectively. Long service medals existed in Canada (243), Australia (247), New Zealand (251) and other territories also (245, 249, 250). In Australia, for instance, silver meritorious and long service medals were issued by its territories before Federation; all had basically crimson ribbons but with stripes in different colours (244). A light blue stripe was present on the ribbons of Queensland and a pink stripe on those of Tasmania. The ribbon of the Long and Efficient Service Medal of Victoria had a 14 mm white stripe in the centre (248).

The Permanent Forces of the colonies of the Cape of Good Hope and of Natal were granted a Long Service and Good Conduct Medal (246) with orange and yellow stripes on their ribbons.

In 1910 a new medal was instituted as a replacement for all the above described long service awards and appropriately was called the Permanent Forces of the Empire Beyond the Seas Long Service and Good Conduct Medal (242) which in turn became obsolete in 1930 when it was replaced by the British Army medal (Plate 29, 209).

The Police and the Fire Brigade Long Service and Good Conduct Medals (253, 256) were adopted in 1951 and 1954 respectively, while the African Police Meritorious Service Medal (263) was created already in 1915 for native policemen, and superseded by a new medal instituted in 1934. In this year some new awards were created for the Colonial Police (254, 257, 261) and for the Colonial Fire Brigade (260) in a new effort for standardisation. The ribbon of the Ceylon Police Long Service and Good Conduct Medal (262) should not be confused with that of the Special Constabulary Faithful Service Medal (70) illustrated on Plate 24. Finally, members of the Burma Police received medals for distinguished service from 1940 to 1947 when Burma became independent (264). Recognition was also given to the Royal Canadian Mounted Police (255), Malta Police (258) and Sarawak Police (259).

Royal Household Long and Faithful Service Medals

Queen Victoria introduced the first of these awards which, incidentally, should not have had a suspension ribbon; instead a Royal Stewart tartan ribbon was attached to the medal (265). The ribbon, however, cannot be worn on its own. A Long and Faithful Service Medal was issued to eligible members of George V's household staff, usually attached to the second ribbon illustrated (267). An obsolete King George V type is also shown (266). Similar medals were granted on the same terms by the succeeding monarchs, George VI (268) and Elizabeth II (269, 270).

Good Shooting and Other Medals

The first marksmanship medal was introduced in 1869 and until 1883 was granted yearly to the best marksman in the British Army. This tradition was renewed in 1923 and the award now is known as the Queen's Medal for Champion Shots (271). A similar award also existed in India (274) and since 1953 a silver medal is awarded each year to the Best Shot in the Royal Air Force (272).

The Royal Observer Corps Medal (273) and the Cadet Forces Medal (276) were both instituted in 1950: the former is awarded for twelve years' service in the Royal Observer Corps and all ranks, men and women, can be eligible for this award. Officers, warrant officers and chief petty officers who served for twelve continuous years with the Cadet Forces, starting from September 1926, receive the latter medal. Clasps and Silver Roses identify, as usual, succeeding spells of service.

Plate 31. Other Medals

The ribbons illustrated in this plate belong mainly to civilian awards and many are not worn as service ribbons, as the medal with its suspension ribbon is worn in all circumstances.

The King's Medals for Service and for Courage in the Cause of Freedom (277, 278) were instituted in August 1945 to reward foreigners who gave tangible support to the British and Allied cause. The Medal for Courage could have been awarded, for instance, to those who helped escaped British prisoners of war. Members of the crews of Lloyds' ships could receive Meritorious Service Medals (279) in silver and in bronze for acts of courage leading to the saving of a vessel from hazards at sea, and a Service Medal as a reward for irreproachable service. The first award was created in 1893 and the other in 1913, both are attached to the same ribbon. In 1940 another medal was instituted by the Committee of Lloyd's as a recognition for acts of bravery at sea, during the war (280).

The Albert Medals were life saving awards which became obsolete in 1971. The Albert Medals for Gallantry in Saving Life at Sea, of 1st and 2nd Class (281, 285) were instituted in 1866 while the Albert Medals for Gallantry in Saving Life on Land, of 1st and 2nd Class (282, 286) were created in 1877. In 1904 the width of the ribbons of the 2nd Class awards was increased from 16 mm to 35 mm (283, 284) and in 1917 the class distinction was replaced by the following denominations:

Albert Medal in gold for Gallantry in Saving Life at Sea
Albert Medal for Gallantry in Saving Life at Sea
Albert Medal in gold for Gallantry in Saving Life on Land
Albert Medal for Gallantry in Saving Life on Land

A number of institutions have awarded life saving medals during the past years and some medals are still issued currently. The Royal Humane Society issues three medals: the Stanhope Medal in gold (288), and silver and bronze versions also (289, 290). The Coast Line Saving Corps Long Service Medal (291) was instituted in 1911 for the benefit of the volunteer members of the then Rocket Life-Saving Apparatus Companies or Brigades. Twenty years of good service is one of the conditions of eligibility for this medal, which is considered a King's medal and therefore can be worn on the left side of the breast.

The National Life-Boat Institution issues medals in gold, silver and bronze (292) and the Board of Trade issues different life saving medals to British subjects (293) and to foreigners, to the latter with a plain crimson ribbon. The gold and silver medals of the Shipwrecked Fishermen and Mariners Royal Benevolent Society (295) are worn attached to a 25 mm dark blue ribbon, not to be confused with the other blue ribbons illustrated in this plate.

The Hong Kong Plague Medal (294) was given in recognition of relief work during the plague of 1894 and although a number of British servicemen received it, the medal could not be worn on the uniform. Eligible members of the staff of the Queen Alexandra's Imperial Military Nursing Service were issued gold, silver and bronze badges, all with the same ribbon (296) while another ribbon (297) identified reserve personnel.

The London County Council has awarded a number of medals, the ribbons of which have been illustrated: the Medal for Bravery (298) is a reward for acts of courage performed by members of the London Fire Brigade. Firemen can also be granted the awards of the British Fire Services Association, depending on the merit involved, bravery, meritorious service, or twenty, or ten years' service.

The Royal Society for the Prevention of Cruelty to Animals has a Life Saving Medal (306) and a Meritorious Service Medal which hangs from a white ribbon with dark blue edges. The Voluntary Medical Service Medal (310) is awarded for fifteen years' service, with a clasp for each succeeding five years.

The Badge of the Order of the League of Mercy (311) was established in 1899 for members of the League who distinguished themselves by their support of hospitals and charitable work. Members of the St John Ambulance Brigade who served during the 1899–02 war in South Africa were eligible to receive a bronze medal with the typical ribbon of the St John's Order (312).

A commemorative medal was issued in 1910 to coincide with the

Unification of South Africa and was given to civilians and military personnel alike (313).

People's Republic of Hungary

Plate 32. Orders, Decorations and Medals

All the present Hungarian service ribbons are rather small, only 22 mm × 10 mm in size, contrary to the suspension ribbons which are 40 mm wide, to be folded in a triangular pattern, following a tradition set during the late Austro-Hungarian Empire. The only straight ribbon worn is attached to the star of Hero of Socialist Labour (1), the highest award in the country, which is worn in all circumstances, above all other decorations or service ribbons.

The Order of Merit of the Hungarian People's Republic (2), as were the other following orders, was created in 1953 and confirmed by a Decree of 1963; it has one class which could be awarded to the military and to civilians for contributions in promoting Socialism, peace and international co-operation. The Order of the Flag of the Hungarian People's Republic (3) is reserved for civilians only and the star of the order, without a ribbon, is worn on the left breast. This order has three classes with stars of varying sizes; that of the 2nd Class has been illustrated. The star of 1st Class is 82 mm in diameter and has red rubies in place of the berries in the wreath; the same class of the order can also be awarded 'with gems' instead of the rubies to individuals who have achieved exceptional merits.

The insignia of the Order of the Red Flag (4) and of the Order of the Red Flag of Labour (5) are similar, and the ribbons are identical. The former is a military order while the second is a civilian order and the flag on its insignia is plain red, without the red, white and green edging of the former. The red ribbons of the Order of the Red Star (6) and of the Order of Labour (8) are also exactly the same but, once again, one is a military and the other is a civilian award, and in this case their insignia are different. The Order of Labour has three classes, with gold, silver and bronze insignia.

The Order of Merit for Outstanding Services (7) is another award reserved for personnel of the armed forces, as indeed crossed rifles are present at the base of its insignia.

The Medal for Merit in Sport of the Hungarian People's Republic (9) can be awarded in gold, silver and bronze: as with many other Hungarian awards technically it is not a medal as it depicts a small national flag in the centre of a red enamelled star, surrounded by a wreath. Similarly the Medal of Merit for Service to the Country (10–12) in gold, silver and bronze classes, consists of a red flag, with serrated red, white and green edges, above crossed light machine-guns resting on a laurel wreath. The Medals of Public Security (13) and the Fire Brigade (14) consist also of very attractive insignia, in gold, silver and bronze. The commemorative Medal of the Flood (15) is a conventional round medal made of bronze.

Four Medals of Merit for Good Conduct (16–19) are awarded to Army and Air Force personnel and are made of metal and enamel while civilian personnel working with the armed forces (Honvedélm) receive different all metal conventional medals. The latter and Army personnel are eligible for a medal after ten, fifteen, twenty and twenty-five years of irreproachable service, while airmen receive the award after 200, 350, 550 and 800 hours flying. The years of service, or the hours of flying, are inscribed on the medals.

Plate 33. Orders, Decorations and Medals

The awards illustrated in this plate, although relatively modern, are all now obsolete.

The first pattern of the Order of Merit of the Hungarian People's Republic (20) was divided into five classes and the recipients of four classes were entitled to wear a breast star as well. A small replica of the breast star was attached on the ribbon of the insignia, as illustrated, as a means of class identification, because there was only one insignia for all the five classes. A still smaller replica of the star was worn on the service ribbon as well. Breast stars on gold background represented the 1st and 2nd Class, that of the former was 70 mm in diameter while the other was smaller. The background of the 3rd Class star was in silver and a red star only, without background, was worn by recipients of the 4th Class of this order. The insignia only, without extra stars, was worn by recipients of the 5th Class. A Medal of Merit (27) in three classes, was affiliated to this order and consisted of the red star only with the central device in gold, silver or bronze, according to class.

The Kossuth Order (22) had three classes, the first two with a breast star as well as the insignia. The Hungarian Freedom Order (23) consisted of a ten-pointed star in silver or bronze, with Kossuth's effigy in its centre. The ribbons of the old Good Conduct Medal of Merit (25) and of the Medal for Merit of Labour (26) were suspended by the same ribbon and were even similar in appearance although one was a military and the other a civilian award. Both were made of light blue enamel with a surrounding silver wreath: in the centre of the military medal there was the emblem of the republic with two crossed light machine-guns below, while the workers' medal had a hammer crossed with an ear of wheat below a red star.

Another workers' decoration, but of superior standing, was the Order of Merit of Socialist Work (24) and a medal was instituted in 1957 to commemorate the Workers' and Peasants' Rule (29). The 1848 Centenary Medal (28) bears the effigy of Peter Sandor, a national hero of independence. The Flood Medal (30), first issued after the Danube's flooding, was different from the latest one, although the ribbon is the same. The first one depicted a man walking in the water while holding a small child; the later medal shows a man engaged in building, or perhaps strengthening, a dam. The Danube flows in the foreground.

Empire of Iran

Plate 34. Orders, Decorations and Medals
These are the ribbons of the modern Iranian awards and medals; unfortunately, despite all my efforts, I have been unable to obtain information on all those illustrated regarding dates of institution, the significance of their titles and the reason why they were awarded.

The Zolfagher Order (1) is the highest Iranian award and its insignia are worn on a sash and on the breast. It consists of a five-pointed star superimposed on crossed scimitars on a background of golden rays issuing from the centre. While the insignia of the order are made of enamel and precious stones, the medal is made of gold and hangs from a plain ribbon, 40 mm wide.

The gold, the gilt and the silver medal (4–6) are all connected with the Order of Sepah (3) as the gold medal bears the same effigy on the obverse, as the Sepah Medal; the obverse of the gilt and silver medals depict two crossed scimitars and a crown above a wreath.

The Medal for Merit (8) has the same motif as the Order of Merit (7), in blue and red enamels as illustrated, but on a medal. The insignia of the Order of Honour (9) has been illustrated: the Medal of Honour (10) depicts the star, but with one point upwards with the gold Imperial Crown on red circular background only.

The 28th Amordad Medal (14) obviously refers to a date as it is also known as the National Uprising Medal. The two following commemorative medals recall the 25 Years of the Emperor's Reign (15) and the Coronation of the Emperor and Empress (16) of Iran.

Kingdom of Italy

Plate 35. Orders
Centuries before the 1861 Unification, orders and decorations were issued by the independent states of the Italian peninsula but, as service

ribbons were not used then, we will concentrate on the awards instituted by the House of Savoy, which became the awards of modern Italy.

The titles conferred upon the members of an Italian order, usually in five classes, are as follows:

Grand Cross (Cavaliere di Gran Croce)
Grand Officer (Grande Ufficiale)
Commander (Commendatore)
Officer (Cavaliere Ufficiale)
Knight (Cavaliere)

The Knight of the Grand Cross wears the badge of the order attached at the ends of a sash and wears another badge, mounted on to a star, on the breast. The Grand Officer wears the badge of a necklet and a small star on the breast, the Commander has only the neck badge and the badges of the 4th and 5th Class are worn on the left breast, like medals.

Small metal crowns are worn attached to the service ribbon in order to identify the class of an order; three, two and one gold crowns are worn by the three top classes respectively, a silver crown identifies the Officer while the Knight wears the plain ribbon, as demonstrated in the case of the Order of the Crown (6–10).

The Supreme Order of Our Lady of the Annunciation (1) was instituted in 1362 by Amedeus VI, the Green Count. The statute of this order was modified several times, lastly in 1869 by a Royal Charter which defined the rules which still govern this order. The members of the order, in one class only, are granted the title of cousin of the king and there can be no more than twenty members, excluding the king, his family and foreigners, usually sovereigns and chiefs of state.

The Knights wore a gold collar and the badge (placca), which originally was embroidered in gold wire. There were two collars, a large one for special occasions and a smaller one for ordinary use. The scene of the Annunciation i.e. the dove, the angel and the Virgin Mary, forms the centre of the badge and in gold, surrounded by entwined Savoy Knots, it hangs from the collar. A miniature replica of the badge's centre-piece was worn on the crimson service ribbon.

Amedeus VIII, first Duke of Savoy, retired to monastic life in the Castle of Ripaglia where, in 1434, he instituted the Order of St Maurice which was merged with the Order of St Lazarus in 1572 (2). Later, in 1793, King Victor Amedeus III created the cross of the Saints Maurice and Lazarus for the benefit of army officers and gold and silver medals for rank and file, later replaced by awards of the Military Order of Savoy (3). This order was founded in 1815 by King Victor Emmanuel II who, after the fall of Napoleon, had just returned to the throne of the Kingdom of Sardinia. It was modified in 1855 and has existed in five classes since 1857 as a reward for acts of bravery and exceptional services rendered by members of the Armed Forces.

The Civil Order of Savoy (4) was instituted in 1831 as a one class order (Cavaliere) rewarding exceptional acts and services in public administration, in the literary field, arts and public education.

The Order of the Crown of Italy (5) was established in 1868 to commemorate the annexion of the Veneto, in the North-East, which completed the unification of Italy. The order's title refers to the Iron Crown, depicted in the centre of the insignia, with which the kings of Italy were crowned. The Iron Crown is still preserved in the cathedral of Monza.

The Order for Merit of Work (11) and the Star for Merit of Work (12, 13) were instituted in 1901 and in 1923 respectively. The former rewards managerial achievements in the field of agriculture, industry and commerce and its members, one class only, are known as Knights of Work, while the Star for Merit was, and still is, awarded to lower contractors and workmen who become Masters of Work. The ribbon of the latter was initially yellow.

The Order of the Roman Eagle (14) was created in 1942 for the benefit of foreigners, usually Germans, to whom the King did not intend to give any more royal orders. It was divided into a civil and a military division; the ribbon should have been half yellow and half crimson, edged by the national colours, green, white and red on both sides but crimson ribbons with yellow side stripes were adopted instead.

The Colonial Order of the Star of Italy (15) was created in 1914 as an award for native subjects and, exceptionally, it was conferred upon Italians residing in the colonies. It was divided into five classes.

The first medal of Italian Unity (16) was created in 1883 for those who had fought for the country's unification from 1848 to 1870 and another medal was issued in 1922 with the dates 1848–1918 and later yet another one with the dates 1848–1922.

After the occupation of Albania, in April 1939, the King of Italy also became King of Albania and therefore Grand Master of the Albanian orders. The Order of the Besa (17) and the Order of Skanderbeg (18–22) were kept in existence, although their insignia were modified, as a reward for Albanians and Italians residing in that country. Both were divided into five classes identified on the service ribbons by small helmets of Skanderbeg in gold or silver, as illustrated, following the Italian custom. The Order of the Besa (of Fidelity) was a military award while the other order rewarded various merits of civilians and soldiers. Georg Kastriota Skanderbeg (1414–1467) the Albanian national hero, led the rebellion that drove the Turks out of Albania.

Plate 36. Decorations

Gold and silver medals for valour were instituted by Victor Amedeus II in 1793 to reward acts of bravery accomplished by junior officers and other ranks. The recipient of such medals received double pay. However, these awards became obsolete during the period of French rule, and although they were reintroduced in 1815, they were replaced in the same year by the new Military Order of Savoy, the awards of which initially rewarded the rank and file, as well as the officers.

Gold and silver medals with a blue ribbon were again created by King Carl Albert in 1833 and the bronze medal was issued in 1887 to all the soldiers who had received an honorary mention for their valour during the campaigns fought since 1848. The recipients of a gold medal received an annual bonus of Lire 100 and those who had a silver medal, Lire 50. In 1848 the bonus was doubled, and in 1918 it was extended to the recipients of bronze medals as well: Lire 800 yearly for a gold medal, Lire 250 for a silver medal and Lire 100 for a bronze medal. The colonial troops received different medals for valour, with an inferior bonus.

The old nineteenth century ribbons were only 32–33 mm wide, but after 1900 wider, 36–38 mm ribbons came into use and the suspension, initially a metal ring, was replaced by a fixed support known in Italian as 'maglietta'.

The Medal for Military Valour was awarded in gold, silver and bronze (23–26) to personnel of the Royal Army and little five-pointed stars in gold or silver on the service ribbon identified the first two medals. The plain blue ribbon was worn in lieu of a bronze medal.

The gold and the silver medal for Naval Valour (27, 28) were created in 1836 and the bronze one (29) in 1888. The medal for Aeronautic Valour, in gold, silver and bronze versions (30–32) was instituted in 1927. The Naval and Air Force medals are identified by distinctive ribbons, gold and silver medals by stars on the service ribbons as already described. Gold, silver and bronze medals for Civil Valour (33–35) were awards reserved for civilians.

Each succeeding award of the medal, or of the War Cross for Military Valour (41) was identified by an individual service ribbon and a sword was worn on the ribbon of the latter to distinguish it from the ribbon of the War Cross of Merit (37), adopted in 1918. Indeed there are two war crosses although both have the same obverse (36) but one bears the inscription Valore Militare and the latter Merito Militare on the reverse. A Royal Decree of December 1942 ruled that second and succeeding awards of the latter should be identified by small metal crowns (38–40), as listed below on the suspension and service ribbons of the first cross:

1, 2, 3 Bronze Crowns	2, 3, 4 succeeding awards
1, 2, 3 Silver Crowns	5, 6, 7 succeeding awards
1, 2, 3 Gold Crowns	8, 9 and 10 succeeding awards

No one, however, seems to have taken any notice of this decree and individual crosses and ribbons were worn for each award.

The Orient Cross (42) and the Railways War Cross (46) were decorations of World War I. The medal for Field Valour (47) was never issued although specimens of its ribbon could be found. The Fascist War Cross (43) was an unofficial award and the Cross of the Spanish Campaign (44, 45) was awarded during the Spanish Civil War 1936-39.

Plate 37. War Medals

The first and second ribbon illustrated are British and French respectively awarded to Italian soldiers during the Crimean War (48) and the 1859 War of Independence (49). The following medal was created in May 1860 by the Council of Palermo to commemorate the expedition of Garibaldi and his thousand men, which led to the liberation of Sicily and southern Italy (50), and, as in the Campaign of 1870 (51), Rome was taken, the ribbon is crimson and yellow, the heraldic colours of the city. A silver medal later was issued to those who participated in the Wars for Independence (52): clasps with laurel leaves and year's dates were worn across the suspension ribbon (1848, 1849, 1855-56, 1859, 1860-61, 1866, 1867, 1870).

After unification, Italy commenced its period of colonial expansion and each new venture was commemorated by an appropriate medal. However, the conquest of Eritrea (53), the international expedition to China (54) and the Italo-Turkish War (55) by which Lybia was gained, were soon followed by World War I. As the annexion of Trento and Trieste was a relevant Italian purpose for joining in the conflict and therefore this also was a war for unification and independence, the ribbon of the 1915-18 Medal (56, 57) was the same as that of the Wars for Independence Medal, but inverted, i.e. it starts with the green instead of the red. Metal or embroidered silver stars were worn on the service ribbon for each year of participation of the recipient while bronze clasps with laurel leaves and year's date were worn across the suspension ribbon (1915, 1916, etc.).

Similar clasps, but made of silver were attached to the suspension ribbon of the Italo-Turkish War Medal, while plain, straight clasps with the campaign's name and date were worn on the ribbon of Eritrea (Spedizione 1887, Dogali 1887, Campagna d'Africa 1887, Saati 1887, Campagna d'Africa 1888, Saganeiti 1888, Campagna d'Africa 1887-88, etc.).

The 1915-18 War Volunteers (58, 59) received a bronze medal with crimson ribbon and the Volontario Irredento (60) applied a small enamel badge on the ribbon: it depicts the heraldic emblems of Trento, Trieste and Zara. The Inter-allied Victory Medal (61) was adopted soon after the war, followed by a medal commemorating the annexion of Fiume (62), now Rijeka, in Yugoslavia.

The Fascist Campaign (63) was followed in October 1922 by the

March on Rome (64) and the advent of Fascism. The Ethiopian Campaign (65, 66), started in October 1935, was ended in May 1936. The troops participating in the offensive from Somaliland wore a different ribbon (66). The bronze sword with laurel leaves of the War Cross for Military Valour, was worn on both ribbons. The War Volunteers (67) were awarded a medal identical to the previous medal for volunteers but with the initials A.O.I. (Africa Orientale Italiana) in place of the date MCMXV-MCMXVIII, and a different ribbon. Subsequently a medal was issued to commemorate the institution of the Italian Empire, it was the Inter-allied Victory Medal with a new ribbon (68).

A number of ribbons commemorate the Italian participation in the Spanish Civil War: there was a medal for the Italian Legionnaire (69) and another medal, with two ribbons for the War Volunteers (70, 71), the second ribbon was adopted after World War II. There are four different variations of the ribbon of the commemorative Spanish Campaign Medal (72–75) although some of these could be Spanish ribbons.

Italy entered World War II in June 1940 and the commemorative War Medal (76) technically represents the period 1940–43 only, because another medal was issued for the period 1943–45, known as the Liberation Campaign (83). However, the usual bronze clasps dated 1940, 1941, 1942, 1944 and 1945 can all be worn on the suspension ribbon of the former medal. Stars, as usual, replace the clasps on the service ribbons of both medals. The ribbon of the War Volunteer Medal (77) has the colours of the appropriate war medal's ribbon in its centre.

The June 1940 battle on the Western Alpine Front was commemorated by two souvenir medals with white and red ribbons, known unofficially as the ribbon of the French Campaign (78). The Albanian Campaign Medal (79), the Cross of the Italian Expeditionary Corps in Russia (80) and the African Campaign Medal (81) commemorate other stages of Italian participation in the war. The latter ribbon was intended for Italian and German troops, the former would wear it starting with the green while the Germans had narrower ribbons that should have been worn starting with the black. A black and red unofficial ribbon appeared after the war to commemorate service in the Armed Forces of the Italian Social Republic of 1943–45 (82).

Plate 38. Long Service and Seniority Awards

These awards have been divided under separate titles only in order to simplify this text but, in fact, all are long service awards.

The Mauritian Medal (84) for fifty years of military service was created in 1839 for officers of the Armed Forces members of the Order of the Saints Maurice and Lazarus. The generals wore a gold medal on a neck ribbon, while officers had a smaller medal on the breast.

The officers and N.C.O.s of the Royal Army (85) and of the Customs Guards (86) were entitled to 'Long Command' awards, while 'Long Navigation' and 'Long Aerial Navigation' awards were given to the Naval and Air Force officers and N.C.O.s respectively. No device was worn on the blue and white striped ribbons of the Army and Customs, while gold, silver and bronze anchors were pinned on the Naval ribbons for twenty, fifteen and ten years of service respectively (87–89). Miniature replicas of the pilot's badge were used on the service ribbons of the Air Force (90–92).

The following have been titled seniority awards because all were awarded for Anzianita' di Servizio, and were available to all ranks. The Seniority Cross of the Army (93) showed the years of service for which it was awarded in Roman figures on the reverse but the plain service ribbon was always worn, without any device. There was only one Seniority Cross of the Fascist Militia (94) for ten years of service, with a bronze sword on the service ribbon (95) but later, during the war, when twenty years of service were reached a red painted sword was pinned on to the ribbon instead, also on the suspension ribbon (96). There were awards for personnel of the Public Security (97), for the Police in Italian Africa (98), etc.

Commemorative Medals and Crosses of Military Formations

It was the custom in Italy to commemorate the existence of military formations with the striking of medals, often very beautiful and very prized by collectors; for instance the series of regimental medals of World War I. All these are technically only souvenir medals without ribbon, and only those of the major formations, with ribbon, can be dealt with in this chapter. Most commemorate the armies of World War I (102–109), such as the Cross of the famous Third Army (104) made of white enamel with the Lion of St Mark in its centre: the ribbon of the Sixth Army (107) shows British, French and Italian colours as foreign divisions also belonged to this army in 1918. The Eleventh (110, 111) was an army of World War II and its motto and the date of its formation are engraved on the back of the cross.

The 28 Marzo (112), Tevere (113) and Freccie Nere (114) were divisions of the M.V.S.N., the Fascist militia, the latter was in action in Spain.

Plate 39. Medals of Merit and Other Awards

Medals, stars and crosses were awarded to civilians, and often to servicemen who had achieved special merits in various fields. However, most of these ribbons were in existence at different times and, further, some ribbons of minor commemorative medals have been added as well in order to save space.

The Meritorious Service Medal for native colonial troops (115) was a military award but many others were given to soldiers as well as to civilians, for instance the medals connected with the earthquakes (130–132) which were also awarded to foreign servicemen who came to rescue the population. Some medals rewarded special merits in the field of public education (117, 118, 137) or propaganda (116). Other medals encouraged the fight against disease (119, 120) or the improvement of public services (121), of agriculture, industry and commerce (126, 127, 128 and 129). Some were awarded for long service and others for special merit.

A bronze medal was given to the mother or widow of the fallen (122, 123) and prolific mothers also had their own award (135) during the Fascist period. There existed a medal of merit of the Red Cross (125) while the previous ribbon (124) belongs to the International Red Cross Association of Geneva and further down on this plate there is a ribbon for nurses, Dames of the Red Cross (144). A yellow ribbon with tri-coloured edges (146) was worn by military chaplains after World War II and a medal was struck in the 1920s to commemorate the 50th anniversary of the foundation of the mountain troops (147).

The alliance of Italy and Germany was commemorated by a blue ribbon with the Italian and German national colours on the sides (148) and when Japan entered the alliance, the Japanese colours were added into its centre (149).

Plate 40. Fascist, Athletic and Other Awards

Meritorious service in the Fascist Youth was rewarded by square crosses with blue enamel in the centre and the initials G.I.L. (Gioventu Italiana del Littorio) or O.N.B. (Opera Nazionale Balilla); the former was 40 mm wide and the latter, for younger members, was only 37 mm wide. A special ribbon, with broken stripes, was attached to these medals and the colour of the stripes identified the age group of the recipient. The Young Fascists, male and female (from 17 to 21 years of age) had black stripes on the grey ribbons (150), the Avanguardisti (13 to 17 years) dark blue stripes (151, 152) and the females of the same age group, the Giovani Italiane (153) light blue stripes. The Balilla (8 to 13 years) and the Piccole Italiane had dark and light red stripes respectively (154, 155).

The 'Dux' camps took place every summer for the benefit of the Fascist Youth and, incidentally, a badge was struck to commemorate each camp and a medal existed for the camp's Capo Centuria (156) and for meritorious attendance at the camps (157). A silver star was added to the latter ribbon for each succeeding attendance at a camp.

Other medals, in gold, silver 1st Class, silver and bronze were awarded as a reward for athletic achievements (158–161) while the star rewarded merit in sporting activities (162).

The ribbons of the G.I.L. Meritorious Medal (163) and of the O.N.D. (164) were similar, crimson with the national colours in the centre or on both sides, respectively. O.N.D. stands for Opera Nazionale Dopolavoro, the working men's clubs organised by the Party. The same ribbon with the initials 'V.L.' (Volontario della Libertà) embroidered in gold in its centre, was used after the war by Volunteers of the Resistance (Italian Republic – 12).

Italian Republic

Orders, Decorations and Medals

After the war all the Fascist awards were abolished although, in practice, they had already become obsolete in 1943 and remained so in the south of Italy ruled by King Victor Emmanuel III. By the referendum of June 1946 Italy became a republic and in the following years the Italian awards were reorganised entirely.

In 1947 the Military Order of Savoy was renamed Military Order of Italy (1–6) and the insignia was modified, chiefly, a wreath replaced the crown, the initials 'R.I.' (Repubblica Italiana) replaced the Savoy Cross and the date 1947 was added to 1855, below the swords. Gold and silver stars replaced the crowns on the service ribbons of all orders.

A law of March 1951 abolished the Supreme Order of Our Lady of Annunciation and the Order of the Crown (8) of Italy which are the property of the House of Savoy, now in exile, and the same law officially ended the awarding of the Order of the Saints Maurice and Lazarus (7). The loss of the colonies made the Colonial Order of the Star of Italy (9) obsolete. However, those who received these orders can still wear them, and their service ribbons now show stars, but they lost the right of precedence in ceremonial protocol.

The Order for Merit of Work (10) and the Star for Merit of Work (11) are still in existence. The ribbon of the Volunteers of Liberty (12), an award for work in the Resistance, carries the initials 'V.L.' in gold, in its centre.

Plate 41. Orders, Decorations and Medals
The abolition of the royal orders created a vacuum and therefore the

institution of other orders became necessary in order to acknowledge civic deeds and merits. The Order of the Star of Italian Solidarity (19), created in 1947 to reward Italians abroad and foreigners whose work was a valid contribution to the reconstruction of Italy, in three titleless classes since 1949, was not sufficient to fill the vacuum. Therefore, the Order of Merit of the Italian Republic (13) was instituted in March 1951.

It rewards scientific, artistic and literary achievements, services in promoting trade, public welfare, outstanding civil and military service and so on. The order is divided into five classes, identified on the service ribbons by small gold and silver mural crowns (14–19).

The Order of Vittorio Veneto (20), in one class only, commemorates the 50th anniversary of the Battle of Vittorio Veneto, in 1918, and was given to surviving veterans.

New rules were applied also to the granting of military long service awards and distinguishing devices were adopted for wearing on the service ribbons.

Stars are now worn on the service ribbons of the 'Long Command' Medals (23, 24, 25) in gold for twenty/forty years and in silver for fifteen years (26), while the plain ribbon identifies ten years of service. Such medals are now granted also to officers and N.C.O.s of the Public Security (Police) (27).

On the ribbons of the Seniority Medals of the Armed Forces (22) and Customs Guards (24) the following devices can be applied:

Gold Star	for 40 years
Gold Mural Crown	for 25 years
Silver Star	for 25 years
plain ribbon	for 16 years

The last two are used by the rank and file only. The rules regulating the Long Navigation and Long Aerial Navigation (26) awards remained the same as before, although the badges for the service ribbons of the latter have been modified.

The emblem of the Republic replaced the royal emblem on the medals for valour and new regulations established that a gold star surrounded by a wreath should be worn on the service ribbons of the gold medals for Valour of the Armed Forces (28, 31, 34), a silver star on the ribbon of the silver medals (29, 32, 35) and a bronze star, for identifying the bronze medals (30, 33, 36). A plain blue service ribbon now identifies the War Cross for Military Valour (41) and stars in gold, silver or bronze, instead of crowns, are placed on the blue and white service ribbons of the War Cross of Merit (40).

The gold, silver and bronze medals for Civil Valour (37, 38, 39) are still awarded and medals for Civil Merit (42) have been adopted as well, in the meantime. The various commemorative and merit medals adopted after the war have the same ribbons as those previously existing under the monarchy, but the edges of the ribbon of the Meritorious Medal of Education and Art (43) have been changed from black to violet.

Kingdom of the Netherlands

Plate 42. Orders, Decorations and Medals
The Military Order of William (1) is the highest Dutch award and was created by William I in April 1815. Although it could be conferred upon civilians it is primarily a military order and can also be awarded to military units as a whole. During the last war, for instance, it was conferred upon the 325th Glider Infantry Regiment and the 504th, 505th and 508th Parachute Infantry Regiments of the U.S. Army. The personnel of these units are entitled to wear the blue and orange lanyard of the order and other units also have been granted the wearing of the lanyard as a special honour. The Military Order of William is divided in four classes: the recipients wear the insignia of the order in the usual manner.

The Order of the Netherlands' Lion (2) was also instituted in 1815: it is a civilian order, in three classes with an additional medal, which could all be awarded also to eligible members of the Armed Forces, and foreigners as well. The Order of the Oranje-Nassau (3) was created in 1892 and is divided into five classes, for civilians and military men alike. The insignia of the latter have additional crossed swords instead of the wreath, which is the background of the civilians' insignia. Medals of Honour in gold, silver and bronze (4) are affiliated to the Order of Oranje-Nassau and a miniature replica of the medal in appropriate metal, is displayed on the service ribbons.

Until World War II, deserving acts of bravery leading to a mention in despatches were identified by a Gilt Crown worn on the ribbon of the Expedition Cross (11) but in 1944 a special decoration was created instead, known as the Bronze Lion (5). It is a bronze cross with the Netherlands' Lion in a circular background in the centre. Second and succeeding awards, as with other Dutch medals, are denoted by Arabic numbers on the ribbon.

A Resistance Cross was issued in 1946 and two years later the East-Asia Resistance Star (6) was created for the benefit of those who actively opposed the Japanese invaders in Indonesia. The ribbon of the Dutch award is also crimson but the orange stripes are placed on the edges. In 1940, Queen Wilhelmina, then in exile, instituted the Bronze Cross (7) and the Cross of Merit (8) and the Flying Cross (9) in 1941. All are decorations for bravery and succeeding awards of the latter are identified by Roman numbers, from 'II' onwards, on the ribbon.

The Life Saving Medal (10) was created in 1822 and the Expedition Cross (11) has been awarded since 1869 to all the participants in important military expeditions and battles. Military service from 1940 to 1945 was rewarded by the Commemorative War Cross (12) of bronze, adopted in March 1944, while those who after the war served in Indonesia received the Star for Order and Peace (13) adopted in December 1947. The New Guinea Cross (14) was instituted in 1964 for service on the island during 1963–64.

Two mobilisation crosses have been instituted: one was given to those conscripted during World War II (15) and the other commemorates the 1914–18 Mobilisation (26) to protect the Netherlands' neutrality. Participants in the Korean War of 1950–53 received the Cross for Right and Freedom (16).

The Officers' Long Service Cross (17) was instituted in 1844 while the N.C.O.s' Long Service Medal (18) has existed since 1825. In the former's case the years of service are shown by Roman figures (XV, XX, XXV, XXX, XXXV and XL) in the centre of the cross and on the service ribbon. The N.C.O.s receive a bronze medal after twelve years, a silver medal after twenty-four years and a gold medal after thirty-six years of service. A small replica of this medal is worn on the service ribbon.

A medal, now obsolete, was given to Volunteers of the Red Cross (19), differing from the Red Cross Service Medal (22) adopted in 1910. A special medal was struck in 1937 to commemorate the Wedding of Princess Juliana (20) and later, in 1948, another medal was issued to mark her Coronation (21). The Cross for the Four Days March (23) is connected with the events which take place at Nijmegen every year in July. The Netherlands Olympic Committee (24) is responsible for the awarding of a special medal, with distinctive blue ribbon, while the Cross for Five Camps (25) is awarded to personnel of the Armed Forces for athletic merits during the military pentathlon.

Kingdom of Norway

Plate 43. Orders, Decorations and Medals
The one and only order of Knighthood of Norway is named after Olaf the Holy, the nation's patron saint. The Order of Saint Olaf (1) was instituted in 1847 by Oscar I and at present it includes three classes, Grand Cross, Commander and Knight; however, as there is also the additional grade of Commander with Star, and that of Knight 1st Class, in practice the order is divided in five classes. An additional Collar may also be conferred, or the order 'with Diamonds' which is another high

distinction. Crossed swords are added to the insignia, below the crown, if the recipient is a member of the Armed Forces. Rosettes and stripes of gold and silver lace identify the classes of the order when the ribbons alone are worn.

The Silver Medal of Saint Olaf (5) was established in 1939 as a reward for civilians and military personnel; awards for military merit are identified by a Silver Branch of Oak Leaves on the ribbon.

The War Cross (2, 3) was instituted by Haakon VII in 1941 and is the highest military decoration for bravery; a small bronze sword is worn on its ribbon and second, and succeeding awards of the cross are identified by additional swords. Its ribbon should not be confused with that of the medal for Outstanding Civic Services (15) which is slightly wider, and has wider white stripes in the centre. A War Medal (8) was created at the same time as the War Cross and up to three gold five-pointed stars can be worn on its ribbon.

The medal for Heroic Deeds (4) is a civilian decoration awarded for life saving and similar circumstances.

Haakon VII instituted the Cross (6, 7) and the Medal of Freedom (11) in March 1945 for civilians and servicemen, Norwegians and foreigners, for exceptional contributions leading to the liberation of Norway. A Bronze Rose is worn on the ribbon of the 1940–45 Participation Medal (9) by those Norwegians who during the war had served their country abroad. The Norwegian contingent in Korea received the last of the war medals in the 1950s (10).

Some important events of Haakon VII's long reign were commemorated by special medals, for instance his 70th Anniversary (12), and his Coronation (14) which took place in 1906. There is also the Haakon VII's Jubilee Medal with clasps inscribed '1905–1930' and '1905–1955' (16) and the King's Commemorative Medal (17) for household staff, with a plain red ribbon.

The King's Medal for Civilian Merit (13) was instituted in 1908 and the same ribbon was borrowed for the 1949–52 Antarctic Expedition.

The Badge of Honour of the Red Cross (19) and other medals exist as well, for instance a Gold Marksmanship Medal (18), a Gold Medal for Athletics, with green ribbon, and a Gold Medal for Marching, with light blue ribbon.

Republic of Poland

Plates 44, 45. Orders, Decorations and Medals
The Order of the White Eagle (1) was instituted in 1921 as the highest

national award for civil and military merits; it had one class and the Knight of the order wore the cross, suspended on a shoulder sash 100 mm wide and the star on the left breast, while the Grand Master wore the collar of the order as his rank's privilege. The President of the Republic was the Grand Master of the Order of the White Eagle.

The Military Order of Virtuti Militari (2–7) was created in 1792 by the last King of Poland, Stanislav August Poniatowski, and approved by the Diet the year after. The order was revived in 1919, with five classes, awarded for outstanding deeds of bravery to individuals and military units. The towns of Lwów and Verdun have been awarded the 5th Class of this order. The 1st Class, or Grand Cross, was represented by a cross attached to a shoulder sash and by a breast star, and was received by Marshals Pilsudski and Foch and by some European monarchs. The 2nd Class decoration was worn by Commanders on a neck ribbon while the Knights of the other classes wore the cross on the left breast as a medal: the cross of 3rd Class was enamelled, that of 4th Class was made of gold and the 5th Class decoration was in silver. Rosettes and stripes of gold and silver lace were used on the service ribbons to identify each class of the order.

The Order of Polonia Restituta (8–10, 13, 14) was also divided into five classes but was primarily a civilian award, although servicemen could also become eligible. It was instituted in 1921. The Independence Cross (11, 12) ranks before the 4th and 5th Classes of the previous order and therefore its service ribbons have been illustrated following this order of precedence. The Independence Cross and the Medal (21) were given to those who distinguished themselves in the struggle for independence before, during and after World War I, excluding engagement in the Polish-Soviet War, for which another medal was awarded. The cross could also be awarded with swords in special circumstances.

The Cross of Valour (15, 16) rewarded deeds of bravery performed during the 1st and the 2nd World Wars; second and succeeding awards are identified by bronze bars with engraved oak leaves and up to four awards can be recorded.

The Volunteer's War Cross (17) was made of steel and had a white enamelled eagle in its centre. Like the Volunteer's War Medal (22), it rewarded voluntary service in the period 1918–21 but as both decorations were instituted in 1939, the outbreak of World War II prevented their award.

The Cross of Merit for Bravery (18) was a decoration for policemen, members of the Frontier Defence Corps and Frontier Guard who distinguished themselves in the performance of duties. It was instituted in 1928 and, second and third awards of this cross were identified by one and two plain silver bars on the ribbon. This amaranth and blue ribbon, but without the diagonal stripe, was originally adopted in 1923 for the

Cross of Merit (20, 24, 27 [Plate 45]), which existed in gold, silver and bronze variations. The same decoration, but with additional crossed swords (19, 23, 25, 26), was revived in 1942 as a reward for war merit. The 1923 version could be awarded four times and gold, silver and bronze plain bars were worn on the ribbon for the second and succeeding awards, while bars with oak leaves identified further awards of the Cross of Merit with Swords. Small crossed swords in gold, silver or bronze were attached on its service ribbons in any case.

Plate 45. Orders, Decorations and Medals
The Army Medal (28) (see also Plate 44) was created in 1945 as a reward for six months of operational service during World War II, or twelve months in a non-operational role. The Navy Medal (29) and the Air Force Medal (30) were awarded under similar conditions and all could be awarded up to four times, identified by bars with oak leaves on the ribbons. A similar award existed also for the personnel of the Mercantile Marine (31).

A special decoration, the Cross of Merit of the Armies of Central Lithuania (32), was given to participants who distinguished themselves during that campaign, in 1920. The Cross of Silesian Valour and Merit (33) commemorates the Silesian uprising of 1921. Originally only a buttonhole ribbon was worn but in 1931 the award was officially approved and a cross was instituted as well.

A silver Life Saving Medal (34) was instituted in 1928 for Polish citizens and foreigners who have saved someone else's life at the risk of their own. Each succeeding award was marked by a bronze star on the ribbon. In the same year another medal was established for the benefit of those who served from November 1918 to 18 March 1921 in the defence of Poland, including civilians and foreigners who aided the Polish Army: this is the 1918–21 War Commemorative Medal (35). The 10th Anniversary of Independence Medal (36) was also created in 1928 while the 3 May Medal (37) was instituted four years earlier, to be awarded yearly on this date.

Gold, silver and bronze Long Service Medals (38–40) all had the same ribbon and therefore Roman numbers in the appropriate metal were worn on the service ribbons to identify the length of service.

The Commemorative badge of the Commemorative Cross of Monte Cassino (42) was awarded to all those who fought at Monte Cassino, Passo Corno and Piedimonte between 12 and 31 May 1944, or Polish soldiers of II Corps who were wounded previously, from 27 April, on the same front and to personnel of the 1st, 161st (former 2nd) and 3rd Field Hospitals taking part in that battle.

The Honour Badge for Wounded (43) consisted of a ribbon in the colours of the Virtuti Militari, with additional metal stars for each wound contracted.

Polish People's Republic

Plates 45, 46. Orders, Decorations and Medals
The Order of the Builders of People's Poland (1, 2) was instituted in 1949 and can only be bestowed upon Polish citizens for distinguished contributions in the field of social work, education, art and culture, health, defence and other fields of national interest. It can also be awarded to institutions, towns, provinces, etc., and has one class only.

The ribbons of the orders following have once again been illustrated in their correct order of precedence; some new orders and decorations were instituted after 1945 but some old ones were revived by the People's Republic and except for minor modifications on their insignia they are still the same as before. The Order of Polonia Restituta (3, 7, 11, 14, 16) and the Order of Virtuti Militari (4, 8, 13, 15, 17) have been joined by the new Order of the Grunwald Cross (5, 9, 12) in three classes, created in 1944, and by the Order of the Banner of Labour (6, 10), in two classes, created in 1949. The former rewards military service in the field or contribution towards the formation and development of the Armed Forces. The Order of the Banner of Work is primarily a civilian award for exceptional deeds in the building of socialism. It encourages the technical progress in the field of industry and social improvements in education, culture, health, etc.

A gold, silver and bronze Cross of Merit (18, 27, 29) can be awarded to civilians for distinguished service or individual achievement and, for instance, it could be given to metal workers, miners and shipbuilders after fifteen, ten or seven years of service, respectively. It could also be awarded to institutions and factories. The Cross of Valour (19) was revived as a military decoration in 1944 and the Medal for Merit on the Battlefield (20, 28, 30) in gold, silver and bronze variations was instituted in 1943. There are two patterns of this latter medal: that for the Battle of Lenino and another one, with the date 1944 on the reverse, for all the other engagements. Members of the Polish resistance received the Partisan's Cross (21) in 1945.

The Medal 'For Your Freedom and Ours' (22) was created in 1956 as a recognition of service on the Republicans' side during the Spanish Civil War. The Silesian Uprising Cross (24) was re-instituted in 1946 and the Greater Poland 1918-19 Uprising Cross appeared in 1957.

The Warsaw Medal 1939-45 (31) commemorates the 1939 defence of this city, the famous uprising of 1944 and its final liberation in January

1945. The Oder, Neisse and Baltic Medal (32) and the Victory and Freedom Medal (33) both commemorate events of 1945, the former was given for service connected with the establishment of the new frontier. The Medal for Self Sacrifice and Bravery (34) is a new life saving award created in 1960, as previously such acts were rewarded by the Cross of Merit.

From 1951 to 1960 the Armed Forces Long Service Award (35–37) was given in gold for fifteen years service, in silver for ten years and in bronze for five years but later the bronze decoration was discontinued and only gold and silver awards were granted for twenty-five years and fifteen years respectively.

Plate 47. Medals and Honour Badges
Since 1960, fifty years of successful wedlock are rewarded by the Long Marriage Medal (39–40), a charming white metal medal with two roses on a pink central background.

The ribbon of the Berlin Medal (41) is followed by those of the gold, silver and bronze Defence Service Medal (42–44). The latter has the same ribbon as the Fire Service Medal (48, 52, 56) and the same devices are used on the service ribbon of both to identify gold and silver awards, while plain ribbons are worn by recipients of bronze ones. The Country Youth Award of Merit (45) has an original horizontally striped ribbon, green with the national colours in the centre.

The Janek Krasicki Badge (46, 50, 54), the Honorary Badge of the Polish Red Cross (47, 51, 55) and the Flood Fighting Badges (49, 53, 57) are all awarded in gold, silver and bronze and devices in gold and silver are worn on the service ribbons of the first two.

The breast star of the Order Virtuti Militari, 1st Class and its 115 mm sash ribbon complete the illustrations of this chapter (58). Except for some minor details of manufacture the difference between this insignia and the pre-1943 pattern is that the Polish Eagle has lost her crown.

Imperial Russia

Plate 48. Orders, Decorations and Medals
A great number of decorations and medals existed in Russia before the Revolution but there was not a great variety of ribbons because the ribbons of the orders of knighthood were used for the majority of medals as well.

Saint Andrew was the protector saint of Russia and appropriately the Order of Saint Andrew, created by Peter the Great in 1698, was the highest in the country. It had one class only, of Knight, who wore the badge on a collar and a sash, and the star of the order on the breast. Special awards were made occasionally of badges and stars studded with diamonds. The ordinary badge of the civil division has been illustrated, together with a section of the order's sash ribbon, 100 mm wide (1); military awards were identified by additional crossed swords below the top crown of the badge (2).

The recipient of the Order of Saint Andrew automatically became a member of the orders of Saint Alexander Nevsky, Saint Anne, Saint Stanislav and of the Order of the White Eagle.

The Order of Saint Catherine (3), in two classes, was established in 1714 to be bestowed only upon ladies. The order was named after the martyr Saint Catherine of Alexandria and its institution was inspired by Catherine Alexseyevna, second wife of Peter the Great.

In 1725, soon after the death of Peter the Great, Empress Catherine instituted the Order of Saint Alexander Nevsky (4), of one class, for officers of the Army and Navy. Catherine II, the Great, instituted the Order of Saint George (5) in 1796: this order was divided into four classes and was essentially awarded for bravery, although until 1833 the 4th Class was a long service award. The 1st Class of the order was usually given to victorious high commanders, while since 1855 the 4th Class was awarded regardless of rank and position. Therefore, also privates were eligible for outstanding valour in the battlefield.

The Order of Saint Vladimir (6, 7) was also instituted by Catherine II, in September 1782, on the twenty-fifth anniversary of her reign. Basically it was a reward for long service with exceptional merit but could be given for bravery as well. It had four classes.

The Order of Saint Anne (8) was founded in 1735 by the Duke of Schleswig-Holstein whose son became Peter III, Emperor of Russia. In 1797 the Order of Saint Anne became officially a Russian order, divided in three classes, and a 4th Class was added to the order in 1815. The Order of Saint Anne could be bestowed upon officers, civilians and members of the clergy.

The Orders of Saint Stanislav (9) and of the White Eagle (10) were originally Polish and were entirely taken over by Nicholas I after the Polish insurrection of 1831. The Order of the White Eagle was founded in 1325, reinstituted in 1705 by August II of Poland and, after the annexion of the Duchy of Warsaw by Russia, the Russian Emperor continued to bestow it upon the Poles. The badge of the order consisted of an eagle, similar to that of the Saint Andrew's order, with the Polish Eagle, upon a cross superimposed on its chest. The Order of Saint Stanislav was founded in 1765 by Stanislav August Poniatowski, King of Poland. It had three classes and was awarded for distinguished service performed by officers or civilians of special merit.

The Order of Merit in Agriculture (11) was created in 1913 in one class only, as a reward for exceptional merits in the field of agriculture. A Russian version of the Order of Saint John of Jerusalem existed also; it was founded in 1797 in the reign of Emperor Paul I and was abolished in 1917. A white enamelled Maltese cross topped by a crown, with the usual black ribbon, was the insignia of the order.

In 1929 the cousin of the late Nicholas II created the Order of Saint Nicholas the Miracles Worker for the benefit of Russian World War I veterans in exile. The white, yellow and black of the ribbon are the colours of the Romanov House (14).

Classes of some of the above described orders carried the right of hereditary nobility, for instance the 1st Class of the orders of Saint Anne and Saint Stanislav and minor decorations, such as crosses, medals or badges were affiliated to some orders as well. The Saint George Cross was instituted in 1807 as a bravery decoration for N.C.O.s and privates and in 1856 the award was reorganised in four classes. A Medal for Bravery, later known as the Saint George Medal, was created in 1878 and was in four classes, as with the cross. The recipients of a cross or a medal received an annual surpay according to the class of the decoration they possessed. A different Medal for Valour was instituted by Catherine the Great and later, after 1878, yet another medal in four classes was issued to the other ranks. All the above described awards were attached to the ribbon of the Order of Saint George.

The first campaign medal was issued in 1706 for the capture of Kalish, in Poland. It was attached to a light blue ribbon of the Order of Saint Andrew and the same ribbon was used for successive medals, until 1774, when a Saint George's ribbon was attached to a medal commemorating the peace treaty with Turkey. The latter ribbon was used as a suspension for the medals of the four successive campaigns against Turkey and Sweden until 1790, when a ribbon of the Order of Saint Vladimir was used for the medal commemorating the peace treaty with Sweden.

In 1806 the crimson ribbon of the Order of Saint Alexander Nevsky was attached to medals awarded for the liberation of Georgia and the Saint Vladimir's ribbon was borrowed for a Chaplain's Cross instituted in 1814. In the same year Paris was captured after the defeat of Napoleon and, twelve years later, a medal was issued to commemorate this event: its ribbon was evenly divided between the light blue ribbon of Saint Andrew and the colours of Saint George's ribbon (12), orange and black.

This trend was repeated in 1828 when a medal was given to participants in the Persian War and its ribbon was half in the colours of the Order of Saint George and half of the Order of Saint Vladimir. Ribbons half of Saint Andrew and half of Saint Vladimir were introduced in 1850 (Pacification of Hungary and Transilvania Medal) and a combination of Saint George's and Saint Alexander Nevsky's ribbons appeared ten years later (Subjugation of Chechen and Daghestan Medal).

Subsequently, this type of ribbon became quite common and at this point I can only suggest to the keen student of Russian history to acquire the book *Russian Orders, Decorations and Medals* by Robert Werlich, which explores this subject in depth by illustrating and describing all the Czarist medals and ribbons, and the Soviet awards as well. Over eighty medals have been instituted since the beginning of the eighteenth century to commemorate all the events of the period until the outbreak of World War I.

A bronze medal with a red, blue and white ribbon was issued to all those who participated in the organising of the 1896 Census of the population (13) and later, in 1907, a medal with white, orange and black ribbon was given to survivors of the Far East Naval Expedition under Admiral Rozhestvenski, which took place during the Russo-Japanese War.

In the following years a few medals were created to commemorate the anniversary of bygone battles and wars, and the medal for the 300th Anniversary of the Romanov Reign, with white, yellow and black ribbon was issued in 1913. Four years later the Revolution closed this chapter of Russian history.

Union of the Soviet Socialist Republics

Plate 49. Orders and Decorations

After the October Revolution all the former Imperial awards became obsolete and in time new awards, of different conception, were gradually established. Soviet ribbons are usually only 24 mm–25 mm in width and as medals' suspension they are mounted in the typical Russian crossed pattern on a metal plaque. The medals are worn on the left breast in the usual manner, and they are placed so that the left side of the ribbon of the first covers the right side of the second ribbon and so on, thus achieving an even, overlapped appearance.

Stars of Hero of the Soviet Union and of Socialist Labour are always worn well above all other decorations and medals, or above the service ribbons, as for instance could be observed in photographs of cosmonaut Yuri Gagarin, who received both. Marshal Zhukov wore an impressive number of service ribbons but on his bluish-green parade uniform of the 1950s he only had his four stars of Hero of the Soviet Union and the two stars of the Order of Victory just below. Service ribbons are 10 mm in length.

The star of Hero of the Soviet Union (1) is the highest award and the gold star with its suspension ribbon is worn in all circumstances. Although the award was instituted in 1934 as a citation only, the star and its red ribbon were created five years later. Similarly, the Star of Hero of Socialist Labour (2) was first issued in 1940 although the award had existed as a citation only since 1938. The Order of Lenin (3) is given concurrently with the two previous decorations and recipients of second awards have an inscribed bust placed in their home town, while recipients of a third award of Hero of the Soviet Union or of Socialist Labour, combined with a third decoration of the Order of Lenin are entitled to a bust placed in the Palace of the Soviets, in the Kremlin. The Order of Lenin was instituted in April 1930.

The Order of the October Revolution (4) was created in 1967, the 50th anniversary of this event. The order of Victory (5), instituted in 1943, is the highest military award and has been conferred only eight times for brilliant acts of leadership. General Eisenhower and Field-Marshal Montgomery are among the recipients.

The Order of the Red Banner (6) is the oldest in the Soviet Union as it was created in 1918; it is a military award for individuals and for military formations and, as with all the previous awards, has one class only.

During World War II some new military awards were instituted in order to strengthen the determination to fight the invaders of Russia and, adding to national pride, they were named after the great leaders of the past. These awards were worn on the breast in the form of stars, made of gold, silver and enamel.

The Order of Suvorov (7-10) and the Order of Kutuzov (11-14) were each divided in three classes and given to army officers as a reward for personal contribution in the planning and execution of successful field operations. Alexander Vasilevich Suvorov was one of the greatest military leaders of all times. He was born in 1729, joined the Army as a private and eventually, in 1800, he became Commander-in-Chief of the Russian Army. Field Marshal Michael Kutuzov achieved fame during the wars against Napoleon and was responsible for the defeat of the latter's army in Russia.

Plate 50. Orders and Decorations
The Order of Usjakov (15-17) and the Order of Nakhimov (19-21) were instituted in 1944 as a reward for naval officers; junior officers, petty officers and seamen could be awarded the Usjakov (18) and Nakhimov Medals (22). Feodor Fedorovich Usjakov (1744-1817) and Paul Stephanovich Nakhimov (1802-1855) were famous Russian admirals. Bogdan Khelnitsky was an illustrious Cossack leader of the seventeenth century and a military order was dedicated to him in 1943 (23-26); it had three classes which could be awarded to officers and other ranks of the Army,

Navy and partisan forces. The Order of Alexander Nevsky (27) had only one class, and was created in July 1942.

The Order of the Red Star (28) was instituted in 1930 as a reward for exceptional merits and could be awarded in peace- and war-time to military personnel and also to civilians.

Silver medals for Valour (29) and for Meritorious Service (30) were created in 1938 for officers and other ranks alike.

Plate 51. Orders and Decorations
The Order of the Patriotic War (31–33) is another World War II award, instituted in 1942, for the benefit of all ranks of the Armed Forces, including partisans. It had two classes, with gold and silver rays, respectively, as background to the decoration. The Order of Glory (34) had three classes, with all gold, gold and silver and silver stars, all three attached to the same ribbon which is the obsolete one of the Order of Saint George. It was awarded to the other ranks of the Army and to Junior Lieutenants of the Air Force for acts of bravery.

The Order of the Badge of Honour (35) and the Order of the Red Banner of Labour (36) are civilian awards adopted in 1935 and 1938 respectively. The Star of Marshal of the Soviet Union (37) was first awarded in 1940 and consists of a gold star, studded with diamonds, which was suspended by a red ribbon (38) around the neck. The Supreme Marshals and Marshals of Corps became eligible for this decoration in 1943 but their stars were smaller, had no diamonds and were suspended by coloured ribbons (39–43).

Plate 52. Medals
The Medal of the 20 year Jubilee of the Red Army (44) was issued in 1938 and initially was attached to a 24 mm red ribbon which was changed to a grey ribbon with red edges in 1943. Subsequently, a new Jubilee Medal was instituted after every ten years (45–47): these medals are issued to all ranks on active service at the time of the anniversary.

Special medals were instituted for partisans in 1943. A silver medal (48) was given for exceptional acts of bravery and a bronze one (49) rewarded lesser deeds and meritorious service. Both were attached to light green ribbons with a red and a blue stripe respectively. The medals for Valiant Labour (50), for Heroic Work (51) and for Distinguished Labour (52) were all civilian decorations, the first and the last instituted in 1938, while the medal for Heroic Work was granted in 1945 to workers whose exceptional individual war-time efforts deserved a tangible recompense from the nation. The Order of Glory of Motherhood (53) was given, in three classes, to mothers of nine, eight and seven children respectively. An enamelled white and blue ribbon is part of the decoration.

A number of 'Defence' medals were awarded from 1942 onwards to military personnel and civilians who took part in the major defensive battles of World War II. The medals for the Defence of Leningrad (54), Odessa (55), Stalingrad (56) and Sevastopol (57) were instituted in December 1942, while the medals for the Defence of Moscow (58), the Caucasus (59) and the Arctic (60) were created in 1944. The Medal for the Defence of Kiev (61) was issued in 1961. The background colour of most of their ribbons is olive green.

The Victory over Germany medal (62) was instituted on 9 May 1945 and the Victory over Japan medal (63) on 30 September 1945; they were issued to all the members of the Armed Forces who had taken an active part in the military operations on these two battle fronts.

Plate 53. Medals

As the victorious Red Army spread into Eastern Europe some medals were given to commemorate the 'Capture' of enemy capitals or the 'Liberation' of allied capitals. These medals were all instituted in June 1945 and were made of bronze. Belgrade (69) was liberated in October 1944 and Warsaw (68) in January 1945; Budapest (64) was captured in February and Koenigsberg (65) and Vienna (66) on the 10 and 13 April respectively. Berlin (67) was captured on 2 May 1945 and Prague (70) was liberated on the 9th of the same month.

In 1965 the war veterans still serving in the Soviet Armed Forces received the 20th Anniversary of World War II medal (71), a bronze medal suspended by an original ribbon, two thirds red with an 8 mm bi-coloured edge. As two crossed ribbons are the usual suspension of the medal the green and black edges are placed on the outer sides, leaving the red in the centre.

The Good Conduct Medals (72–74) were instituted in 1958 and are awarded for twenty, fifteen and ten years of excellent service to all ranks of the Armed Forces.

The Centenary of Lenin Medal (75) was created in 1970 to commemorate the 100th anniversary of his birth. Many other medals have been given since the end of the last war to reward services rendered and at the same time to encourage production and efficiency during the years of post-war reconstruction (76–80). Two such instances are the medal for the Restoration of the Mines in the Donets (76) which was created in 1947, and the medal for Reclaiming of Virgin Lands (81).

A medal issued in 1947 commemorated the 800th Anniversary of the Foundation of Moscow (83) and ten years later another medal was instituted to commemorate the 200th Anniversary of the Foundation of Leningrad (84).

United States of America

Plate 54. Decorations

The United States service ribbons are usually 35 mm wide and, since the late 1940s, they all measure 10 mm in length. Previously the U.S. Navy and Marine Corps regulations required the ribbons to be ½-inch in length while Army ribbons were ⅜-inch in length. The change in size was approved by the Secretary of the Navy on 30 April 1948 and the option to wear ½-inch ribbons ceased in October 1951 when the ⅜-inch (10 mm) size became mandatory uniform regulation.

Airmen of the U.S. Army Air Force (now U.S.A.F.) were bound by Army regulations, those of the U.S. Navy, Marine Corps and Coast Guard followed their own respective rules.

The Medal of Honor (1) is the highest decoration and has different pendants for soldiers, sailors and airmen, all worn with the same ribbon. The decoration of the Army has been illustrated.

The naval Medal of Honor was authorised by Congress in December 1861 to 'be bestowed upon such petty officers, seamen, landsmen and marines as shall most distinguish themselves by their gallantry in action and other seamanlike qualities'. The army Medal of Honor was adopted in 1862. Both decorations were made of bronze, in the shape of a five-pointed star with its upper point downwards: the centrepiece depicted Minerva repulsing the allegorical figure of Discord. The naval pendant and the army pendant were attached on to the ribbon by means of an anchor and of a trophy (cannons, sword, cannon-balls and the American Eagle) respectively. The ribbon was straight, initially blue at the top, with thirteen alternate red and white stripes in the bottom half. In 1896 the colours were changed to red, blue and white (similar to Great Britain's 185). The rules for awarding these decorations were also revised a few times.

The present army Medal of Honor was adopted in 1904 while the naval decoration took the form of a cross pattée after World War I and reverted to the original pattern in 1942.

The Medal of Honor of the U.S. Air Force is rather similar to that of the Army although the suspension piece is different and a portrait of the Statue of Liberty is shown in its centre.

The Congressional Space Medal of Honor (28) was instituted on 29 September 1969 to reward astronauts who in the performance of duties have distinguished themselves by exceptionally meritorious efforts and contributions to the welfare of the nation and of mankind. It is worn on the breast, suspended by a straight uninspiring ribbon, which is not in keeping with the great deeds it is intended to reward.

The Brevet Medal (3) was founded in 1921, awarded to holders of brevet commissions given by the President and confirmed by the Senate for distinguished conduct on the battlefield.

The Navy Cross (2) and Distinguished Service Medal (6) were authorised in February 1919 while the Distinguished Service Cross for the U.S. Army (4) and the Medal (8) were authorised the year before. Airmen were eligible to receive Army decorations and medals before the U.S. Air Force became an independent service in 1947. The Air Force Cross was authorised by Act of Congress in July 1960.

The distinguished service crosses are awarded for acts of heroism involving the risk of one's life, while the medals reward meritorious service rather than bravery. The Certificate of Merit (5) has been awarded to soldiers and N.C.O.s since 1847 and a medal has been issued with the certificate since 1905. However, from 1918 to 1934 the recipients of the Certificate of Merit, on application, could have the certificate exchanged for a Distinguished Service Medal and, after 1936, they received the Distinguished Service Cross instead.

The Specially Meritorious Medal (11) was given to all ranks of the U.S. Navy and Marine Corps who distinguished themselves other than in battle during the 1898 war against Spain. It was authorised in March 1901.

The Legion of Merit (12–15) was established by Act of Congress on 29 July 1942 and could be awarded in any of its four degrees to members of the Armed Forces. The Chief Commander wears the badge pinned on the left breast pocket, the Commander has the badge attached on to a ribbon, worn around the neck, the Officer's and the Legionnaire's badges are worn as medals, with a suspension ribbon. A small golden replica of the badge is worn on the suspension ribbon of the Officer while the ribbon of the Legionnaire is plain. Small badges are worn on the service ribbons of the first three degrees as means of identification.

The Silver Star (16) was instituted in 1918, the Bronze Star (23) in 1944. The former is a gallantry decoration of the Army, conceived in order to replace the silver citation stars previously worn on service ribbons, and rates after the Distinguished Service Cross. The Bronze Star is strictly an Army award as airmen of the U.S. Army Air Force were given the Air Medal (27) instead. It rewards acts of heroism (24) of a lesser degree than required for the Silver Star or meritorious achievement and service less than required for the Legion of Merit. The Soldier's Medal (17), established in 1926, rewards acts of heroism 'not involving actual conflict with an armed enemy'.

The Distinguished Flying Cross (18) was also instituted in 1926 and is awarded to aviators of the armed forces who distinguished themselves by heroism or extraordinary achievement while participating in aerial flight.

In the case of the Army and Air Force, succeeding awards are shown on the ribbon by bronze oak-leaf clusters; sailors, marines and coast guardsmen wear gold stars instead.

The Airman's Medal (19), Coast Guard Medal (20) and the Navy-Marine Corps Medal (21) all rank in precedence with the Soldier's Medal already described.

The original Purple Heart, which was technically called the Badge of Military Merit, was instituted by General G. Washington in 1782 but only three awards were made. It was a heart-shaped purple velvet badge with silver embroidered edges.* During World War I small gold 'V' chevrons were worn on the right forearm by men wounded in battle but this custom was superseded in 1932 by the introduction of the Purple Heart medal (29).

The Distinguished Service Medal (7) is the highest decoration of the Merchant Marine, followed by the Meritorious Service Medal (30) and by the Mariner's Medal (22), and were adopted, respectively, in 1942, 1944 and 1943. The latter rewarded personnel who suffered wounds or illness as a result of enemy action.

The Meritorious Service Medal was instituted in 1969 as a reward for outstanding non-combat meritorious achievements and it ranks in between the Legion of Merit and the commendation medals. The National Security Medal (31) was instituted by Executive Order in 1953 and can be awarded to any person, regardless of nationality, including members of the Armed Forces, for 'distinguished achievement or outstanding contribution in the field of intelligence relating to the national security'. The Medal of Merit (26) is a civilian award.

Only one example of each second-award badge has been illustrated: succeeding awards are denoted by additional oak-leaf clusters on the service ribbons of the U.S. Army and Air Force, by gold stars on those of the U.S. Navy, Marine Corps and Coast Guard. Bronze oak-leaf clusters stands for a second and succeeding individual award and, since 1943, a silver oak-leaf cluster identifies the owner of five consecutive awards. The letter 'V' device stands for 'Valor'. On the ribbon of the Bronze Star the oak-leaf cluster and the 'V' device can be worn together, providing that the latter are attached to the inner side, left, and the cluster on the outer side.

Plate 55. Medal of Freedom, Commendations, Citations and Other Awards

The Medal of Freedom (32, 33, 34, 35) is a civilian decoration introduced in 1945 to reward meritorious acts or service as efforts in the contribution

*The National Geographic Magazine's Insignia and Decorations of the United States Armed Forces – 1943.

of the war against the enemy. It could be awarded to citizens and members of foreign Armed Forces and to U.S. citizens whose acts were performed outside the boundaries of the United States. There are four degrees of this decoration, identified by metal palms on the ribbon.

The Distinguished Civilian Service Medal (45) was instituted in 1956: as it is purely a civilian award its lapel button, instead of service ribbon, has been illustrated.

The Navy Commendation (37) was authorised in January 1944, the first of a series of similar awards for all the services. Initially it consisted of a letter of commendation signed by the Secretary of the Navy and was shown on uniform by the ribbon only; later a medal pendant was added to the ribbon. The Army Commendation Ribbon (38) was granted in December 1945, later to become Army Commendation Ribbon with Medal Pendant and, later still, in 1960, it was redesignated Army Commendation Medal. The Reserve Special Commendation was founded in 1946 to reward meritorious command of units of the Navy and Marine Corps Reserve, for four years, from 1930 until the beginning of World War II.

From 1947 members of the Coast Guard, previously entitled to the naval award, were granted their own Commendation Ribbon, now a medal (39). The Air Force Commendation Medal (40) and Joint Service Commendation Medal (36) were authorised in 1958 and 1963, respectively.

Second and succeeding awards are identified by oak-leaf clusters for soldiers and airmen and by gold stars in the case of sailors, marines and coast guardmen. The 'V' device could also be worn on the ribbons. The achievement ribbons rank after the commendation ribbons: The Secretary of Transportation Commendation for Achievement (44), formerly awarded by the Secretary of the Treasury, is shown by a ribbon only; the one illustrated is an embroidered specimen.

The Presidential Unit Citation emblems originated in 1942. The emblem worn by soldiers and airmen (49) was called Distinguished Unit Badge and the former wear it above the right breast pocket, while airmen wear the same badge, but smaller, amongst the other service ribbons. Oak-leaf clusters can be worn on this badge and small bronze stars on the naval emblem (43).

Bronze stars are also used in lieu of succeeding awards on the Navy and Coast Guard Meritorious Unit Commendation (46, 48) while a small silver sea-horse is always present on the Gallant Ship Citation Ribbon (53) of the Merchant Marine. A gold letter 'N' was worn on the ribbon of the Navy Presidential Unit Citation to U.S.S. Nautilus for its sub-polar expedition, and a bronze globe was awarded to U.S.S. Triton.

Personnel who took part in the operation for which the unit received its citation are entitled to wear the ribbon, also if transferred to other units, while personnel who later became part of such a unit wear the ribbon for the duration of their service in that unit only.

The Valorous Unit Award (50) is bestowed upon units for acts of heroism of a lesser degree than required for a Presidential Unit Citation and the Air Force Outstanding Unit Award (47) rewards meritorious service in support of military operations, but not valour. The ribbons of the Philippine, Vietnam and Korean Presidential Unit Citations (52, 54, 55) can only be worn by personnel who originally were part of the unit in question.

The Air Force Longevity Service Award (56) is awarded after four years of active service in replacement of service stripes and succeeding periods are shown by oak-leaf clusters. The Armed Forces Reserve Medal (57) is given to reservists who had served for ten years within a period of twelve consecutive years. The Ten-year device is worn on the suspension and service ribbons for a second award. In the same manner, bronze stars are worn on the ribbons of the Naval and Marine Corps Reserve (58, 59, 60). The first ribbon is that of the Organised Marine Corps Reserve Medal as a reward for only four years' service: it was authorised in 1939. There is no medal for the latter, which was awarded from 1945 to 1965, later replaced by the Armed Forces Reserve Medal. There is no medal for the ribbons of the Air Reserve Forces, Navy Reserve and Coast Guard Reserve Meritorious Service which are given after four years of 'excellent' service; naval and coastal succeeding awards are identified by bronze stars. The Air Force Small Arms and Expert Marksmanship Ribbon is the counterpart of the naval marksmanship ribbons on Plate 58.

Plate 56. Service Medals

Medals given to those who honourably took part in the campaigns of a war are called 'service medals' because they are intended to reward service performed by combatants and non-combatants alike.

Naval and Army medals for the same campaigns are often different from each other, although usually they are suspended by the same ribbon: further, some medals were awarded only to Army personnel, or to Naval personnel only and it should be remembered that until after World War II the service ribbons worn on Naval uniforms were larger than those of Army personnel.

There are two Civil War medals (65, 66), one for the Army and one for the Navy: they were authorised in 1907 and 1908 respectively. The medal for the Indian Wars was authorised in 1907, to reward service in campaigns fought from 1865 to 1891 (67). The Spanish Campaign Medal for the Spanish American War 1898–99 (68) came into being in

1905 and the service medal of the same war (69) in 1918. Most of the pre-World War I campaigns were a consequence of the war which led to the occupation of Cuba and Puerto Rico in 1899–1902; medals were issued in 1915 and 1919, respectively (70, 71). The Army of Cuban Pacification Medal (75) was given to men who served on the island from October 1906 to April 1909. There was also a Navy version of the same medal.

The Philippine Congressional Medal (72) was an Army award, while the Philippine Campaign Medal (73) had army and naval versions: the Army medal was given for service from 1899 to 1913 and was authorised in 1905, while the other was authorised in 1908 for service from 1899 to 1903.

The China Campaign, or China Relief Medal (74) was established in 1905. The Mexican Service Medal commemorates the Mexican Campaign 1911–17 (76) and was issued in 1917 while the Mexican Border Medal (80) contrary to the previous was an Army only medal, for service in 1916–17, issued the year after.

In the meantime the Navy had taken part in three campaigns for which medals were struck: the 1st Nicaraguan Campaign (77) for which a medal was authorised in 1913, the Dominican Campaign (78) had its medal in 1921 and another medal, issued in 1917, commemorates the Haitian Campaign (79) 1915–16, while a later issue of the same medal commemorates service in 1919–20.

World War I was remembered by only one medal, the Victory Medal (81, 82): the following battle clasps could be worn on its suspension ribbon:
- Cambrai
- Somme, Defensive
- Lys
- Aisne
- Montdidier-Noyon
- Champagne-Marne
- Aisne-Marne
- Somme, Offensive
- Ypres-Lys
- St Mihiel
- Meuse-Argonne
- Vittorio-Veneto
- Defensive Sector

The following, also worn on suspension ribbons, were service clasps:
- England
- Siberia
- Italy
- Russia
- France

These clasps were made of bronze and a bronze star on the service ribbon replaced each battle clasp, but not service clasp; citations were identified by silver stars.

The Army of Occupation Medal (83, 84) originally issued had a ribbon with a wavy blue edges, but this ribbon was soon changed for the second one illustrated.

The 2nd Nicaraguan Campaign Medal, the Yangtse and China Service Medals (85, 86, 87) were all issued by the Navy and worn by seamen and marines who took part in those operations. The Navy and Marine Corps Expeditionary Medals (89, 90) reward war operations on foreign soil and succeeding medals are represented by bronze stars. Personnel involved in the defence of Wake Island in December 1941 wear a silver 'W' on the service ribbon of their Navy Expeditionary Medal. In the early 1960s both medals were replaced by the Armed Forces Expeditionary Medal (Plate 57, 110).

The American Defence Service Medal (88) was awarded in 1941 for twelve months' service between 8 September 1939 and 7 December 1941. The possession of a foreign service clasp was identified by the wearing of a bronze star on the service ribbon. Personnel of the Navy, Marine Corps and Coast Guard sailing in war operational Atlantic waters were entitled to a small bronze letter 'A' which, however, could not be worn together with stars on the same service ribbon.

Three theater of operations medals were established by Executive Order of the President in November 1942, they are: The American Campaign Medal (91) for those who served in the American Theater of Operations, and bronze stars on the service ribbon are awarded for certain operations; The European-African-Middle Eastern Campaign (92) and the Asiatic-Pacific Campaign Medal (93) on the service ribbons of which silver and bronze stars and bronze arrowheads could be worn.

The ribbons illustrated at the bottom of this plate were all adopted in May 1943 to identify the service of merchant seamen who had traded in the same waters as their armed counterparts and were, after all, subjected to the same hazards. Three ribbons (bars) identified zones of operations (94, 95, 96); The Combat Bar distinguished merchant seamen actually involved in war operations (97), with stars to denote the abandonment of one's ship, while the Defense Bar (98) was awarded for service between 8 September 1939 and 7 December 1941.

Another two Merchant Marine ribbons have been illustrated in the next plate.

Plate 57. Service, Good Conduct, Polar Medals, etc.

The Women's Army Corps Service Medal (99) was instituted in 1943 for service in the Women's Auxiliary Corps from 20 July 1942 and later in the W.A.C. until September 1945.

After the World War II Victory Medal (100, 101) had been issued in 1945, the Merchant Marine issued its own (102) in the following year and, in the same year, the Army of Occupation Medal (103) was authorised. There is a version for the Army and Army Air Force and another version for the Navy, Marine Corps and Coast Guard, both using the same ribbon. The Berlin Airlift device is a miniature of a C-54 aircraft, worn on the suspension and service ribbons by those who participated in the Berlin airlift from 26 June 1948 to 30 September 1949. However, in July 1949 the Medal for Humane Action (104) was approved for the same purpose.

The National Defense Service Medal (105) was authorised in 1953 to reward honourable active service from 1950 to 1954 and the Korean Service Medal (106) was awarded for war service in Korea during the same period. Two United Nations medals (107, 108, 109) are also affiliated to that war.

The Armed Forces Expeditionary Medal was founded in 1961 to be awarded to personnel of the Armed Forces participating in operations for which no service medal has been authorised, for instance the 1958 expedition in Lebanon, the operations in support of Nationalist China, operations of assistance to Laos, Thailand, etc. Bronze stars on the ribbon identify succeeding awards. Bronze stars are also present on the ribbon of the Vietnam Service Medal (111) and identify the successive campaigns of that war. The Merchant Marine has also adopted a service bar (112) for seamen who served in Vietnamese waters.

The Combat Readiness Medal (113) was authorised in 1964 for personnel of the Air Force, aircrew members, who are combat-ready for a period of four years, second and succeeding awards are denoted by oakleaf clusters in bronze.

Good conduct medals rank before all the service medals and are awarded to enlisted men only. The Navy medal (114) was the first to be issued, in 1869, but the present pattern was re-designed in 1892, bronze and silver stars identify succeeding awards. The Marine Corps Good Conduct Medal (115) was authorised in 1896 and originally bronze Arabic numerals were worn on the service ribbon for further spells of service, but now stars are used instead. The Coast Guard Good Conduct Medal (116) was authorised in 1923 and stars are used on its service ribbon as well. The Army Good Conduct Medal (117) was instituted in 1941. According to regulations only one medal can be issued and clasps or devices denote succeeding awards: a second award of the Army Good Conduct Medal is identified by a bronze clasp with two loops, a third by three loops and so on; the sixth award, given after eighteen years of service, is identified by a silver clasp with one loop. There are silver clasps with up to five loops (thirty years' service) and gold clasps with from one to five loops, the latter identifying up to forty-five years of good conduct.

The Air Force Good Conduct Medal (118) was adopted in 1963 and the medal is the same as that of the Army but with a different ribbon. Succeeding awards are identified by bronze and silver oak-leaf clusters.

In 1943 three ribbons were adopted to reward the efforts of the flyers of the Civil Air Patrol. All were similar in design with the C.A.P. badge in the centre: the one issued for 1,500 flying hours (119) had blue side bands, that for 1,000 flying hours had red bands and the ribbon for 500 hours had green bands.

The Dewey Medal (120) and the Sampson Medal (121) commemorate the Battle of Manila Bay and the naval engagements in the West Indies respectively.

The Peary Polar Expedition Medal (122) was awarded in 1944 to members of the 1908–09 Arctic expedition of Admiral Peary. The later Antarctic expeditions received prompter acknowledgment: Admiral Byrd's expedition of 1928–30 (124) was commemorated by gold, silver and bronze medals in 1930; the Admiral was to receive the only gold medal. Silver medals only were awarded in 1936 to members of the 2nd Byrd Antarctic Expedition (125).

The NC-4 Medal (123) commemorates the first transatlantic flight accomplished by the NC-4 Flying Boat in 1919. As only the seven crew members of the craft received this medal, the ribbon is very rare indeed.

Another Antarctic expedition took place in 1939–41 (126) and the Antarctica Service Medal (127) rewarded military and civilian members of the post-war U.S. installations in the Antarctic. Bronze and silver stars, arrowheads, the wintered-over discs and a miniature Marine Corps badge can be worn on its ribbons. Personnel who had spent one winter on duty in the Antarctic were eligible for the wintered-over clasp in bronze which was worn on the suspension ribbon; for two winters one received a gold clasp and for three winters a silver one. The clasps were replaced by discs on the service ribbon.

The Bailey Medal (128) was established in 1885 to reward yearly one naval apprentice with an outstanding record; the medal was made of gold.

The first two Philippine ribbons (129, 130) were awarded to U.S. personnel who took part in the defence and subsequent liberation of the Islands. The Philippine Independence Ribbon (131) was given to those who served on the Islands, or in their territorial waters, on 4 July 1946. Later the latter was issued to the recipients of the other two also.

The American Typhus Commission Ribbon (132) was given from December 1942 for worthy service in the campaign against typhus.

Plate 58. Life Saving Medals, Marksmanship Medals, etc.
The Lifesaving medals (133, 134) were adopted in 1874 as a reward to any persons who endangered their own lives in the attempt to save someone else's life at sea. The medals are issued in two classes, gold and silver. The second type of ribbons was adopted after World War II (135, 136).

The Navy and the Coast Guard award marksmanship badges and medals to personnel who have distinguished themselves at important shooting competitions. The ribbon alone can be worn in lieu of the badge or medal (139–145).

The American Red Cross is a very complex organisation, divided into different branches, the personnel of which wear various insignia to identify their assignment, rank and length of service. The American Red Cross made its most distinguished contribution in war-time and during World War I a medal (146) was awarded for six months' service in the United States or abroad. A white stripe was added to the medal's ribbon for each additional six months of duty (147–150). During World War II some different ribbons were used to identify length of service reaching back to the 1920s (151–154).

The last medal (155) is purely an item of curiosity: its obverse depicts the bay of Naples and an inscription on the reverse defines it as 'Commemorative medal of the entrance of the Allied Armies in Naples – 1st October 1943'. It is possibly the work of some fast-thinking Neapolitan medals' manufacturer. However, as obviously no time was available for weaving a new ribbon, these medals were sold attached to the ribbon of the former Fascist March on Rome Medal, by then quite obsolete.

Republic of Vietnam

Plate 59. Orders, Decorations and Medals
In this chapter, including in this and in the following plate, all the military awards have been illustrated, many of which were received by military and civilian members of former allied nations, during the Vietnam War. The service ribbons are usually 36 mm × 10 mm in size, made of conventional silk or embroidered with coloured cotton.

Many of these awards derive from the previous awards of French Indochina and others were created later, during the subsequent long war.

The National Order of the Republic of Vietnam (1–6) was awarded to individuals who distinguished themselves with outstanding achievements, exceptional service, sacrifice, heroism, noble attitude, or extraordinary talent that reflect great credit on, or was beneficial to, the country. The order had five classes with conventional insignia and service ribbons with rosettes and stripes of gold and silver lace in the French manner. The ribbon is that of the former Order of the Green Dragon of Annam (France) and the green dragon is still present in the order's insignia.

The Military Medal (7) is primarily a gallantry decoration for N.C.O.s and soldiers but it could be given also for at least thirteen years of honourable service.

The Army (8, 9), Air Force (10, 11) and Navy Distinguished Service Orders (12, 13), each in two classes, are a reward for officers who have been wounded several times and received citations in combat or in the line of duty and could be given to officers who accomplished exceptionally important achievements. Whole units are eligible for these orders and general officers of other armed services also. Rosettes are worn on the ribbons of the 1st Class decorations and both suspension and service ribbons of the Army and Navy orders are particularly beautiful and very original.

The Army (14), Air Force (15) and Navy Meritorious Service Medals (16) were awarded on the same conditions as the previous orders to N.C.O.s, Petty Officers and other ranks. A miniature replica of the Special Service Medal (17) is always worn on the suspension and service ribbon of the medal, which was issued to military personnel and civilians in recognition of exceptional deeds and important missions involving the risk of one's life.

The Gallantry Cross was a decoration for the military, whole units, civilians and civilian organisations accomplishing acts of valour in combat and consequently were cited as follows:

at Armed Forces level	Gallantry Cross with Palm (18)
at Army Corps level	Gallantry Cross with Gold Star (19)
at Divisional level	Gallantry Cross with Silver Star (20)
at Brigade and Regimental level	Gallantry Cross with Bronze Star (21)

Personnel of units cited wear the Gallantry Cross Unit Citation Emblem (22), i.e. the ribbon with palm or stars in a golden frame.

Plate 60. Decorations and Medals

Corresponding decorations existed also for personnel of the Air Force and of the Navy. The Air Gallantry Cross represented citations for bravery in air combat conferred at the level of the Air Force (23), Tactical Wing (24) and Squadron (25) identified on suspension and service ribbons by gold, silver and bronze wings respectively. The three classes of the Navy Gallantry Cross were marked by gold (26), silver (27) and bronze anchors (28).

Eligibility for the Hazardous Service Medal (29) did not entail participation in combat operations but required special conditions involving distinguished service in dangerous circumstances.

The Life Saving Medal (30) was in fact a cross, with a smaller enamelled red cross in its centre and the Loyalty Medal (31) was a star with the word 'Trung', meaning 'loyal', in its centre. Military personnel and government officials wounded in action while fighting the enemy were eligible for the Wound Medal (32), which is a six-pointed star on a gold, ornamental background.

The Armed Forces Honour Medal (33, 34) is a special reward for individuals whose efforts have been a valid contribution towards the organisation, training and development of the Armed Forces. There were two medals, of gold, or 1st Class, and of silver, or 2nd Class, with different ribbons. The titles of the Staff Service Medal (35, 36), Technical Service Medal (37, 38) and the Training Service Medal (39, 40) are self-explanatory and were given to individuals who showed outstanding personal capabilities or rendered special services while performing their duties. These awards are all in two classes, identified by different ribbons only.

The Leadership Medal (41) was awarded to commanders of combat units who displayed excellent leadership in combat; it has five classes according to the grade of leadership involved, i.e. Army Corps, Division, Regiment, Battalion and Company level. There are also five classes of the Military Service Medal (42) for all ranks who have completed their prescribed service with distinction and good conduct. The Air Service (43) and Navy Service Medal (44) have four classes and are awarded on the same conditions.

The Civil Actions Medal (45, 46) is a reward for outstanding services rendered by the military in the field of civil affairs. The medal of 1st Class was for officers and the 2nd Class for the other ranks. Exemplary service and discipline was recognised by the Good Conduct Medal (47), in five classes for all ranks.

The various phases of the Vietnam War were commemorated by the Campaign Medal (48) and by a dated scroll on the ribbon. Vietnamese and foreign civilians whose actions were directed to the improvement of the material and moral welfare of the Armed Forces were eligible for the Unity Medal (49) and the next-of-kin of those who lost their lives in the line of duty received the Medal of Sacrifice (50).

Kingdom of Yugoslavia

Plate 61. Orders, Decorations and Medals
Yugoslavia became a unified nation after World War I (1918) being made

up of Serbs, Croats and Slovenes (Kraljevina Srba, Hrvata i Slovenaca) and a constitutional monarchy in 1921. The name Yugoslavia was introduced in 1931 and the country was composed of two Serbian kingdoms, Serbia and Montenegro and all the countries which were previously under Austro-Hungarian rule (Croatia, Slovenia, Dalmatia, Bosnia, Hercegovina and Voivodina).

As Serbia's was the predominant power in the new nation and the first to have achieved independence, as early as 1878, most of the Yugoslav orders originally belonged to her. A national order, the Order of the Yugoslav Crown (6) was instituted in 1930.

As a general rule, the insignia of the 1st, 2nd and 3rd Class of the orders were worn following the French pattern, the insignia of 4th Class was worn on the second button of the tunic and that of the 5th Class on the left side of the breast but no device was worn on the service ribbons to identify the classes of the orders. If the decoration was with swords (sa macevima), crossed swords were worn on the service ribbon and, second and succeeding awards of the same decorations were identified by gold oak clusters (hrastova grancica). All decorations awarded during a war had a red ribbon.

Only single decorations and medals were worn suspended on an individual ribbon, while the ribbons of groups of orders, decorations and medals were attached to a bar 4 cm wide with a small hook in the centre of each ribbon for hanging its decoration. All the ribbons, except those of the Medal for Military Virtue (8) and the Royal Yugoslav War Cross (Plate 62, 15), were triangular in shape.

The Order of the Karageorge Star (1–3) was the highest in the kingdom; it was instituted by King Peter I in four classes for officers, with and without swords (1904), to commemorate one hundred years of the uprising under Karageorge in 1804, and gold and silver stars for other ranks (1915). Its service ribbon was 30 mm in width, usually red with white side stripes or all red if awarded in war-time. The latter, illustrated, has additional swords and therefore crossed swords would be present on the decoration as well, below the star.

The Order of the White Eagle (4), in five classes with and without swords, was instituted in 1883. On the insignia the swords were worn below the crown; its service ribbon was red with light blue side stripes 28 mm in width and, of course, as was customary, with different wider suspension ribbons. The Order of St Sava (5) named after the founder of the Serbo-Orthodox church, was created in 1883 in five classes and as with the previous order, it was originally Serbian.

The Order of the Yugoslav Crown (6) was instituted in five classes in 1930 and took precedence over the latter.

The first Serbian award for bravery was instituted in Montenegro by Peter Patrovic Njegus in 1841 and later the Yugoslav Medal for Bravery

(7) which, in gold and silver classes, was created in 1913, remained the highest decoration. Its red ribbon was 25 mm wide. The Medal for Military Virtue (8), with its 33 mm ribbon, was established in 1883 and gold and silver medals were created in 1913 to reward Meritorious Service (9). Its service ribbon is only 24 mm wide.

Two similarly narrow ribbons were instituted in 1913 to commemorate the Serbo-Turkish Campaign of 1912 (10) and the Serbo-Bulgarian Campaign of 1913 (11). The medals were made of bronze.

A coronation medal came into being in 1903 to mark the accession to the throne of Peter I (12), and was given to members of the Royal House, Members of Parliament, officers of the Armed Forces and to all the descendants of Karageorge, the founder of the reigning dynasty and commander of the Serbian rebellion of 1804.

Plate 62. Military and Civil Medals, and Decorations of Serbia and Montenegro

World War I is commemorated by two bronze medals: the Liberation and Unification Medal 1914–18 (13) and the Commemorative Medal of Albania (14); both were adopted in 1920.

Prince Alexander, the heir to the throne, instituted the former in the name of the late King Peter I, whose effigy is depicted on the obverse of the medal. The reverse bears the Serbian Eagle and the dates 1915, 1916 and 1917 on the arms of the cross. Many allied servicemen received this medal, which is technically a cross, and the French Government, for instance, officially sanctioned the wearing of it in 1931. Its red, blue and white service ribbon, of Montenegran extraction, is some 3 mm narrower than the ribbon of the King Peter I Medal, but the suspension ribbons of both are exactly the same, 39 mm in width.

The second medal commemorates the Retreat to Albania and was instituted on 5 April 1920. As Serbia ceased to be an independent state in 1918 and, as on the other hand some component states of the Kingdom of Yugoslavia had actually been fighting against the Entente, the Inter-allied Victory Medal could not be adopted.

The last war medal commemorates the 1941–45 conflict and a crown is worn on the ribbon to emphasise that the recipient fought for and under the leadership of the monarchy. The Royal Yugoslav War Cross (15) was established in 1945.

The following three ribbons identify civil decorations. Gold and silver medals for Civil Merit (16) were created in 1902 and subsequently taken over by the Kingdom of Yugoslavia. Their service ribbons were only 20 mm wide. The Red Cross Order (17) was established in 1871 and the Red Cross Medal in 1912 (18).

The Army regulations published in August 1942 state the following

order of precedence for the decorations and medals worn on uniform:
After the last of the orders, St Sava Order, 5th Class:
Gold and Silver Medals for Bravery
King Peter I Medal
Commemorative Medal of Albania
Medal for Military Virtue
Gold and Silver Medals for Meritorious Service
Gold and Silver Medals for Civil Merit
Commemorative Medal of the Serbo-Turkish Campaign 1912
Commemorative Medal of the Serbo-Bulgarian Campaign 1913
Commemorative Medal of the Liberation and Unification 1914-18

Foreign decorations and obsolete orders, decorations and medals of Serbia and Montenegro also could be worn by their recipients. Indeed a number of orders and decorations had been instituted and were subsequently abolished before 1918. The Serbian Order of the Cross of Takovo (19) was created, with its five classes in 1865, and was awarded with swords since 1878. It became obsolete in 1903, together with the Order of Milos the Great, established in four classes in 1898, and that of Queen Natalie, the latter being an award for ladies only, established by King Milan Obrenovic.

The Order of Prince Lazarus was instituted in 1889 to commemorate the 500th anniversary of the Battle of Kosovo and its one class, the Collar was worn by the King and by the crown prince after reaching age. After the Unification, the Order of Prince Danilo (20) instituted in 1852 was also abolished, together with the old (stara) Medal for Bravery (21) and the Obilic Medal (22), the bravery medal of Montenegro, instituted in 1851. The last two medals were dedicated to Milos Obilic, the great hero of independence.

Socialist Federal Republic of Yugoslavia

Plate 63. Military Orders, Decorations and Medals

Unfortunately, not a great deal of information is available on this subject, therefore my efforts are limited to the translation of captions which appear in the illustrated plates.

The highest military awards are the Order of the People's Hero (1), the Order of Freedom (2) and the Order of the Battle Flag (3), followed by the Order of the Partisan Star (4-6) in three classes identified by different badges or, for service dress, by three different ribbons. The same rule applies to the Order of the People's Army (7-9) and the Order of Military Merit (10-12). The latter is followed in order of precedence by the Medal for Military Merit (13) which in turn has four white stripes on its ribbon as the preceding three classes of the order are identified by one, two and three stripes, respectively.

However, the Order of Bravery (14) and the Medal for Bravery (15) have differing ribbons, the latter has a ribbon similar to that of the old Medal for Military Virtue, still present among the modern decorations, but now with a different ribbon (16).

Plate 64. Civilian Orders, Decorations and Medals

The Order of the Yugoslav Star (17) was instituted in 1954 in three classes, awarded for outstanding cultural, political and scientific achievements or special merit towards the cause of international co-operation. Foreign heads of states may be awarded the Order of the Yugoslav Grand Star. Small replicas of the insignia are worn on the service ribbons.

The Order of Hero of Socialist Labour (18) and the Order of the People's Liberation (19) each consist of one class only.

The Order of the Yugoslav Flag (20–22) was created in 1947 and reorganised in 1961: it consists of five classes with conventional insignia, those of the last two classes are worn on the breast, as are medals. Small badges are attached to the service ribbons to identify each class.

The Order of Merit to the People (24–26) and the Order of Labour (27–29) are both divided into three classes identified on the service ribbons by one, two or three stripes respectively. There also exist a Medal for Merit to the People (32) and a Medal for Labour (33) both with four stripes on their ribbons, in accordance with custom.

The Order of Brotherhood and Unity (30, 31) has two classes, with one or two thin blue stripes respectively on either end of their ribbon. Finally, there is a Medal of Merit (34).

Bibliographical Note

Among many useful publications on the subject, I should especially like to mention the following:

Awards of Honour – The Orders, Decorations, Medals and Awards of Great Britain and the Commonwealth from Edward III to Elizabeth II, by Captain A. Jocelyn, C.V.O.

Československé Řády a Vyznamenání by Dr V. Macháček and Lieut.-Col. V. Amort.

Danish Orders and Medals by Capt. P. J. Jørgensen in association with Kai Meyer.

Deutsche Auszeichnungen by Dr K.-G. Klietmann.

Huy Ch'o'ng an Thu'ong Trong Quân-Lu'c Viêt-Nam Công-Hòa.

Imperial Iranian Military Flags, Decorations, Uniforms and Insignia.

Insignia and Decorations of the U.S. Armed Forces, a publication of the National Geographic Magazine.

Medals, Ribbons and Orders of Imperial Germany and Austria, by D. G. Neville.

Orders, Decorations, Medals and Badges of the Third Reich, by D. Littlejohn, M.A., A.I.L.A. and Col. C. M. Dodkins, D.S.O., O.B.E.

Orders, Medals and Decorations of Britain and Europe, by P. Hieronymussen.

Ordery: Odznaczenia – Polskiej Rzeczypospolitej Ludowej, by H. Holder.

Ordery: Odznaczenia, by S. Łosa and S. Bienkowski.

Pour le Mérite und Tapferkeitsmedaille, by K.-G. Klietmann.

Ribbons and Medals by Capt. H. Taprell Dorling, D.S.O.

Russian Orders, Decorations and Medals, by R. Werlich.

United States Military Medals and Ribbons, by P. K. Robles.

For Reference

Not to be taken from this room